For my beautiful children
Daniel and Elke

Dancing

WITH A

COCAINE
COWBOY

Dancing
WITH A
COCAINE
COWBOY

Love and life with a
Colombian drug trafficker

ROBYN WINDSHUTTLE

ALLEN&UNWIN
SYDNEY · MELBOURNE · AUCKLAND · LONDON

First published in 2014

Copyright © Robyn Windshuttle 2014

Allen & Unwin
83 Alexander Street
Crows Nest NSW 2065
Australia
Phone: (61 2) 8425 0100
Email: info@allenandunwin.com
Web: www.allenandunwin.com

Cataloguing-in-Publication details are available from the National Library of Australia
www.trove.nla.gov.au

ISBN 978 1 76011 142 7

Cover and internal design by Lisa White
Set in 12/19.8 pt Chaparral Pro by Bookhouse, Sydney
Printed and bound in Australia by Griffin Press

10 9 8 7 6 5 4 3 2 1

1

I grew up in a weatherboard house in Newport just up the road from the pub, the Newport Arms, a charming Queensland-style building with wide verandas set amid natural bushland. At sunset we kids—my two older brothers, two younger sisters and I—sat atop the grassy mound at the water's edge looking out over Pittwater while Mum and Dad went in for a beer. We'd play, or more often antagonise each other, on the wharf below where fishermen cast their lines and small boats and big yachts anchored for the night.

When the pub burnt down in 1967, it was a big hoo-ha. Everyone in Newport came out to see the fire. It was a hot sunny morning and my dad had just got back from fishing. 'The pub's on fire,' he bellowed, excited and amused all at once. Everyone dropped everything and dashed out. I sprinted barefoot down

Gladstone Street while my brothers shot through Trafalgar Park and down Queens Parade, all of us eager to get the best possie. Kalinya Street was choked with fire engines and photographers and newsreaders with cumbersome handheld microphones. The pub was ablaze, its intense heat keeping spectators at bay. It was a sight to behold. I watched it wide eyed with astonishment from the bus stop across the road outside Reggie Maher's pharmacy, squashed in between adults gasping in horror at the palls of smoke billowing into the sky as the pub went down.

Hordes of people were lured onto the streets another day too, when our entire house was moved. They were curious about this bizarre spectacle. Our house had been hauled from the main drag of Newport along Barrenjoey Road, up to 54a Gladstone Street. It used to sit next to Tyndall's nursery near the surf club and, although it didn't have to go very far, its journey blocked roads and drew a crowd. Mobs of kids and well-wishers milled around as the house was tediously towed up to the battleaxe block opposite the park. I skipped along, excitedly dashing from one side of the street to the other, dodging onlookers, trying to glimpse what would be our new home, my eye on my aqua-coloured bedroom, which looked so bright and breezy.

My two brothers would now sleep in the temporary dwelling, a fibro shack that until then had housed us all: my parents in one room and my two brothers, my younger sister Julie and me in bunks in the middle room. My baby sister slept in her cot at the end of our bunks. It was tiny but somehow Mum managed.

A rudimentary kitchen led out to a primitive laundry where we showered and there was a smelly outside pan toilet which was, in time, replaced when the sewage went on. My parents, my sisters and I would now live in the main house. It had a secret little attic that we girls each used as our bedroom at one time or another over the years. You had to crouch in the attic because the roof was too low, but it offered the most private space in the house and it looked out over our front yard, up the tea-tree lined driveway, and down over our weeping willow trees and the creek where we played, fishing for tadpoles and frogs.

We had a big vegie garden with fruit trees, a beautiful magnolia tree and chooks, whose manure fertilised the garden and whose eggs we collected every morning for breakfast. We ate the chooks on special occasions like Christmas. Dad would chop their heads off on a tree stump, our huge outdoor cutting board, and they'd run around the yard headless for a few minutes before being plucked and thrown into a cauldron of boiling water. There were passionfruit vines and sweet-tasting tomatoes. Next door, at Aunty Pat's, there was a huge mulberry tree with a sturdy trunk and strong branches making it easy to climb and safe to perch, while we gorged ourselves on the berries. Like everyone else on the Peninsula, we spent most weekends getting fried in the sun at the beach with only a smear of zinc to protect our noses. There was either a surf carnival, at which our participation was obligatory as Dad was sweep and captain of Palm Beach Boat Crew, or we'd spend long days at Palm Beach while Dad drilled his oarsmen out to sea beyond throngs of swimmers. He was a hard taskmaster, John Windshuttle, and no one dared disobey him, which earned him the title 'God'. 'Boltar' was another name bestowed on him, for his Viking-like character, by his beloved boat crew. They even gave him a viking copper helmet replete with elk horns. Even though he was respected as an athlete, some people didn't like his arrogance, or brute force, but his skill and drive and passion brought Australian Surf Life Saving to the Royal Palace in London where he and his boat crew met the Duke of Edinburgh himself. At dusk, after a long day in the hot sun, we'd head into the Cabbage Tree Club and hobnob with exclusive members until dark. Some weekends we spent our days swimming and playing at Newport near the pool while Dad dived the reef. Armed with his spear gun and wearing a lead belt and his two olive green lamb's wool sweaters, he'd submerge, his snorkel disappearing from the horizon. And we'd wait. After a while he'd surface with a lobster or three writhing between the sweaters, or a groper and maybe a couple of black fish. On shore, bystanders hovered, impressed and intrigued.

It dawned on me much later in life that while this was the norm for us, most fathers didn't go out and catch dinner for the family. Fresh seafood was always on the table, the staple of our diet. He'd leave at first light, sometimes with me, because I was the only one up at that hour, and return with fresh tailor or bream, which was promptly cooked for breakfast. The sight of Dad hauling in dinner triggered something in some of the male passers-by. Maybe it was the hunter in them and they'd move in, trying to get a closer look, and to throw in their two bobs' worth about the catch—of which my father was completely dismissive. He thought most people were bloody galahs and shunned their praise even though he must have enjoyed the adulation. I certainly gleaned an enormous sense of pride from the admiration he drew from perfect strangers.

Other times we spent long, glorious days at the Basin, an inlet beach across Pittwater from Palmy. The seven of us would clamber into one of our little boats, the *Robyn Anne* or the *Julie Caroline*—my father called his first two boats after his first two daughters—laden with all the picnic paraphernalia and Dad's fishing gear. My mum, Shirley, would usually be in a huff, still cooling off after a fracas with him. Being the super-practical woman that she was—the only way to be with five kids—she'd have the food prepared and the kids organised, ready to get on with the day. And then we'd have to wait, for what seemed like an eternity sometimes, for Dad to finish what he was doing before we could get going.

Most days, bored and frustrated with waiting around, my brother Frank, who loved to stir someone just for the sake of it, would target Jools. She'd start howling and that would lead to sibling spats and whinging, then an almighty roar from 'God': 'Shut those bloody kids up . . . Jesus bloody Christ!' And then it would be on. A major blue, insults, tears, threats, yelling; it was all very dramatic, but eventually my parents settled down and we'd launch at Sandy Beach. My father rowed us over with sheer brute strength, oars creaking in the rowlocks, beads of sweat breaking out on his forehead.

We always took holidays or long weekends at remote, pristine coastal destinations like Seal Rocks or Shoal Bay and I believed we were the only ones who knew about these uninhabited locations. Seal Rocks didn't have any facilities save for a dilapidated hand pump from which we retrieved our water for cooking and showering. From the lighthouse you could see the community of seals huddled together, warming themselves in the sun on the distant rocks out to sea. It was a tiny fishing village then, with one permanent resident, Wal, an old, weather-beaten, grey-haired man who lived rough in a cottage on the beach. He had overgrown yellow toenails from getting about in bare feet all the time and he always smelled of fish. While my brothers surfed the small, beautifully shaped barrels, we girls spent hours scaling the headlands and scurrying through fairytale-like bushlands, dodging pads of cow dung and spying native birds, wallabies, koalas and bluetongues.

I tried surfing at Seal Rocks until one time my brothers saw an opportunity to scare me witless. 'Shark!' they cried. I shot a glance behind me, squinting in the sun, and there I could see the fin. I jumped off that surfboard, swam and then ran for my life towards the shore while my brothers laughed their heads off. It was only a harmless pod of dolphins cruising by but my fear that day put me off surfing for good.

Professional dive crews dived the rocks, hunting sharks. I remember the animosity my father felt towards them for the way they left bloodied carcasses at the shoreline. And I can still see the jaws of their catch hanging on the tent harnesses that lined the beaches like trophies, testaments to their bravery. At dusk, after a whole day waiting for his return, we'd see Dad's boat heading to shore after his day of fishing. Then as lookout—from a precarious rocky outcrop—we'd spot his boat, a speck in the distance, the wake foaming, with Dad holding up three big snapper, or bream, or kingies, his prize for the day.

When we were old enough, Dad would take one of us out on the surf ski with him. I remember sitting between his legs while he propelled along with graceful and rhythmic strokes; it was always a smooth, gliding ride. And he always knew where to fish. It was like he was half fish himself; he had this innate sense. Sitting on the ski, he'd gear up with the lead belt, the spear gun and the flippers and he'd just drop out of sight over the side. I'd sit patiently, sometimes anxiously, on that ski, bolt upright, legs outstretched, waiting for him to surface. The sun blazed down, solid rods penetrating the water so you could see quite a way down through murky seaweed. The silence was deafening save for the high-pitched zing of stray mozzies and the gentle slap of the water against the balsa ski. Sometimes I worried he wouldn't resurface at all. But he always did, and he always had dinner tucked between those sweaters: gleaming, gyrating fresh fish, flipping around in a feverish fit. Dad gutted and scaled them on shore, attracting squawking gulls and other scavengers all competing for the cast offs.

Later in the evening under a starry sky with the sound of waves whispering onto the shore in the darkness, we'd gather around the campfire. Sunburnt and salty, exhausted from a long day of adventures out in the elements, we filled up on the day's catch.

2

*T*he emotional climate at home was not as healthy as our outdoor life. Conflict was part of the routine. My parents fought bitterly and loudly. They were both moody and temperamental and they were deadlocked in a power struggle. Everything was a song and dance, except when they were intimate. Their sex life, as I recall, was the one area where there was peace. Not that I remember any details. Rather, I sensed their physical relationship and understood that it was important to both of them.

My father was arrogant, selfish and dominating; my mother feisty, belligerent and defensive. They were victims of their own miserable childhoods. Mum was born in the Depression to an alcoholic father and a stoic but uneducated mother. Dad suffered a barbaric father and a pitiless, obese mother they nicknamed

'Tiny'. My parents lacked formal education but it was the absence of any emotional intelligence that fed their constant struggle to get their own needs met and which doubtless shaped the emotional development of all their kids.

Dad had a short fuse. He'd order us to 'get this' or to 'get that' or to 'get out of the bloody way'. If you happened to be close by when something he was doing went wrong, he'd explode with frustration and hurl insults, admonishing you just because you were standing there. Like the time he was cooking lobsters in the front yard on an open fire. The cauldron of boiling water got knocked over and all the lobbies spewed out onto the lawn and he absolutely went berserk. He yelled and swore in a filthy rage. I learnt to run for cover before he erupted.

He was abusive, critical and demeaning. He believed that you had to nearly break a person's spirit if they were ever going to develop a strong character. Patience, respect and understanding were nonexistent in his world. Over time, his humiliation and vilification only instilled shame and undermined our self-worth. Mum didn't have the strategies to deal with her burdensome worries and with the logistics of a large family, meaningful interaction was overlooked. Surges of confidence and self-belief vied with self-doubt.

Dad was a violent man too. He bashed my mum a few times, brutally, although he vehemently denied it on the few occasions the police had to be called in. I recall him thrashing her with a thong and her face swelling up after he'd lost his block and belted her again. My mother, unfortunately, agitated rather than mollified. Unwittingly or not, she set up scenarios for ugly confrontations because she had no idea how to defuse a situation and was limited by a complete inability to assert herself. Low self-esteem made her defensive. She thought she had to create elaborate scenes to grab my dad's attention; they never worked. Like the time she discovered lipstick on his grey T-shirt. He'd come home late the night before and had flung the T-shirt onto the floor. I can still see it sitting on their bedroom floor under the open window. It was sunny and the house was in the comfortable disarray of lazy Sunday mornings. He'd obviously been cavorting with another woman and all morning Mum nagged him. She grumbled and snarled, mostly under her breath, but loud enough that we could all hear her in the kitchen, slamming dishes down, seething with anger while he'd lay silently reading his paper in bed, completely ignoring her.

My siblings and I had learnt to gauge the atmosphere. Strangled by the tension that morning, I looked up from whatever I was doing, took a breath and mentally prepared myself for the war that was brewing. We all became fidgety and nervous, anticipating the worst. Dad was infuriated by Mum's behaviour and we knew any moment now he would erupt. And so he did.

Moments later the whole house shook as he bounded out of that bed like a wild animal after prey. Face blue with rage, eyes bulging, he raced after Mum as she bolted towards Aunty Pat's house next door, screaming for her life, Dad in a frenzied pursuit and us kids following. Mum shrieked, 'Pat, Pat! Open the door, Pat!'

She almost made it inside Aunty Pat's. Mum banged that door as loud as she could but it was too late; he grabbed her by the feet and pulled her down. Horrified, we watched as he tore at her hair and neck and dragged her over the damp grass, past flower beds and back through Aunty Pat's garden over the strawberry patch. He punched and kicked, all the while yelling abuse. My eldest brother courageously took a swipe at him but Dad returned an almighty blow, knocking him to the ground. Mum lay bruised and battered, tears running down her blood-streaked face while we hovered there, silenced by the brutality, the smell of fear emanating from us all.

୭୭

We were a big family with big personalities. A survival-of-the-fittest mentality prevailed in our house. No one ever listened to anyone and you had to shout to be heard. I don't remember a civilised discussion ever taking place except when my parents sought help from a marriage counsellor, who advised Dad of the benefits of listening to his family rather than bullying them into submission. So, one night, Dad convened a family meeting and demanded everyone's presence in the living room.

'Sit down, everyone. We are going to have a discussion,' he barked, leaning back in the armchair like lord and master.

'Discussion? About what?' I asked, bemused and sceptical.

'Just shut up and sit down.'

My brothers sighed and raised their eyebrows, but my sisters were too young to get it. We'd never sat down for a discussion before so how could we take him seriously? Mum tried to be supportive.

'Listen to your father,' she said as we sniggered and frowned, wondering why the sudden interest in communication. I just wanted to get back to my homework.

It only took about five minutes before his patience ran out. As usual, when things didn't go his way, he stormed off in frustration, yelling and swearing, hurling abuse, disparaging us all.

Mum suffered panic attacks from the stress. We'd be on a bus, or in some public place, when suddenly she'd take a turn. She swirled with dizzy spells, beads of sweat formed on her brow and her breath came in short bursts. She'd look to me urgently.

'Oh, Robyn, I have to get off the bus,' she'd gasp, shaking. 'Get the girls!'

Dutifully, I would grab my sisters, pull the bus cord and alert other passengers. 'Excuse us, excuse us!' I called out, making our way to the door. Once on the footpath we'd wait silently until she felt better. Then, because I was the eldest, I led, looking ahead while my sisters followed hand in hand behind me.

Those were the days when school kids could go home for lunch. In primary school I used to dash through Trafalgar Park and down our driveway to scoff peanut butter and sultana sandwiches; but when things were really shaky at home I used lunch time as an excuse to check up on Mum. Witnessing her pain and frustration, which on one occasion had her bare breasted and screaming like a mad woman out our front door, rattled us all.

Dad brushed off these highly charged emotional scenes as some sort of joke; in fact, he regarded Mum as some sort of a joke. It never occurred to him to be compassionate, understanding or supportive. And, as always after these outbursts, things would be calm again for a while. My parents would be all lovey-dovey until the next round.

It was an endless cycle that wore everyone down. Neither of them understood the profound impact their troubles had on all of us. Heading off to school after one of their big dramas had us all reeling with stress and uncertainty. We straggled up the driveway in silence, bonded by our silent worry, trying to get our heads past the conflict. It's no surprise our yearly report cards recorded 'disruptive', 'distracted', 'poor concentration'. We were all bright—brighter than most. I, and all of my siblings, possessed a sharp wit, keen intelligence and a strong creative streak, which set us up in the eyes of our peers and teachers as 'colourful individuals'. Sometimes Mum would meet us in the park for lunch near the swings and the slippery dip or she'd pick us up at lunch break in the Fargo Hilton to shuttle us to the beach for a swim during the sweltering summer days. It was her way of settling us and reassuring us that we were loved.

In between all the chaos and emotional upheaval, Mum, who is top heavy in personality, managed to bring comic relief to our lives. Her sense of humour lightened the mood. She taught us to find the silver lining in the worst of grey clouds and it was her sense of the absurd that enabled us to see the funny side of things. Together we laughed, loudly and ecstatically; the sort of bellyaching laughter that released our stress and tightened our familial bond. (Never with my dad, though; he rarely interacted with us and didn't have a sense of humour unless someone was being ridiculed.) We cosied up in front of the black and white telly to watch Bette Davis films and musicals starring Fred Astaire, Ginger Rogers and Shirley Temple. Mum instilled in us this notion that we could do whatever we aspired to in life. She inspired our imaginations and taught us an enormous appreciation of music and the arts. She believed that with talent, passion and commitment you could achieve anything, no matter what your station in life. *There is no such word as can't* was her mantra, and she always encouraged and supported our artistic pursuits. She was also a woman of integrity and drummed into us the difference between right and wrong. *To thine own self be true* was another persistent theme. She offered up these values to us as a survival kit for life. She may have lacked formal education but she was no dummy.

3

*F*rom an early age I yearned to dance. I spun and whirled around our living room through beams of sunlight suffused with dust. At three I made my debut on stage, with my mum, in a physical culture display at Mosman Town Hall. I was the tiniest person on stage and, according to my dad, who, over the years affectionately mimicked my performance that night, I was the most serious, which had the audience in fits of laughter. Apparently I brought the house down with my protruding tummy and forthright march. I have a faint recollection of standing in the middle of that stage and bursting into tears, overwhelmed by the roar of applause, sensing I was the focus of everyone's attention.

As a child, Dad endearingly called me PM: perpetual motion. He was proud of my athletic prowess and boastful to friends and colleagues, likening my form to a greyhound or thoroughbred horse. Just for fun, he regularly pitted me against my brothers to see who could run the fastest. I'd always get a head start and I always won, much to my brothers' chagrin. And then he'd laugh at them, calling them poofters because their little sister had beaten them. He had a cruel streak and derived pleasure from ridicule and belittling. No matter how hard we strived for his approval he rarely gave it and when he did it never came unconditionally, an unhealthy undercurrent of hostility prevailed.

I pestered my mother for years about ballet lessons but wisely she held me back, knowing that if I started too young I would get bored. Then, one afternoon after school when I was six, my sister Jools and I burst into the house hungry for afternoon tea.

'Come and have a look in here, girls,' Mum said, leading us into her room.

Laid out on the bed were two ballet tunics for our first lesson on Saturday morning at a Royal Academy of Dance School in Manly. She'd saved up her child endowment money to pay for them. I could hardly believe my eyes. I was so excited I didn't know if I'd hold out until Saturday.

The school was run by three sisters: Miss Hazel, Miss Vi and Miss Lily. They were old, with purple-rinsed hair and school-marm shoes but Mum reassured me that I'd get quality tuition there—Hazel had danced with Anna Pavlova in her youth. At my very first class, as other students began to congregate on the floor, I walked boldly and confidently straight up to the front and centre, eager to begin. It didn't occur to me to stand back. Miss Gillian, the student teacher, promptly took my hand and led me to the back row.

'I think we'll start you back here with the beginners,' she said.

I was most indignant, stung with humiliation, and looked to my mother for support. She had a smirk on her face and told me, 'Get on with it. You'll be right.' I worked out fairly quickly that this was an open class where the older and more experienced students took their places up the front and the newest students started off in the back.

This was Royal Academy of Dance ballet and I was in Primary Grade. We wore a white linen tunic with a blue belt or a black leotard and pink tights, hair in a tight bun, no wispy bits. Plié, point, lift, point, close, port de bras, gallops, spring points; the first steps came easily to me. I loved it and looked forward to Saturdays every week.

I took to ballet immediately, thriving on the discipline, which was just as well because Hazel was strict. She picked on me a lot, in front of the whole class; she could be quite cruel, like my father.

'Why does she always pick on me?'

'That's because you are talented,' my mum explained. 'She picks on you because you are good, that way you will improve. She's not going to waste her time on anyone who shows no promise, now is she?'

I completed Primary with honours and expected to get first

place in the Grade 1 scholarship. I had no doubt I was going to win, until my mother tipped me off.

'That Jenny is pretty good, Rob,' she said. I hadn't given the possibility that I might not win the slightest thought. Jenny Ludeke was good and she had the classical look: petite, dark hair and prominent facial profile.

'Nah, I'll win,' I replied.

'I dunno, Rob,' Mum murmured.

I was poised on my toes, ready to run forwards to accept my prize and to curtsey when, whammo! Jenny's number was called out. I was mortified. I couldn't openly show how I was feeling of course but I understood even then, at seven years of age, that a sore loser was a poor loser. I stood in line with the other girls while Jenny graciously accepted her prize, inwardly feeling silly and embarrassed that I had even considered myself worthy of first place. Barely a word was uttered between my mum and me during the drive home. I was solemn and disappointed but Mum, who seemed rather nonchalant given my enormous sense of failure, knew this was no failure at all; rather it was a trigger for me either to rise up and meet the next challenge or to give it away.

On my pillow at home I found a present wrapped in pink tissue—chocolates for my performance. Climbing into my pyjamas, I could hear my brothers whispering just outside my bedroom door: 'Did she win . . . did she win?'

I burst into tears and cried myself to sleep.

Saturday was ballet day and an opportunity to get out of the house and away from the strife. As soon as I was old enough, I took the two buses to get to Manly. It meant freedom and independence; it was an adventure but mostly it was time alone in my own space to do my own thing and to dance. I did an open classical class, followed by tap in the smaller studio next door and finally a jazz/performance class back in the big studio. Sometimes after classes I caught the bus up to Woodland Street, Balgowlah, and walked to Ninny's, my grandmother's house in Jackson Street, where Mum and my sisters would meet up with me later in the afternoon. My mum had grown up in this house with her four brothers and two sisters. These days it also served as a refuge when Mum and Dad were at war, even at Christmas time. After an almighty emotional upheaval at home one year, Mum had to drive me and my sisters to Ninny's on Christmas Eve. The next day we waited for our brothers to arrive on the bus so we could all open our presents together.

Ninny's house was a spooky old weatherboard place with a long, dark corridor from the living room to the kitchen. I always hesitated at that corridor. My vivid imagination whipped up a terrifying image of something sinister hovering in the shadows. Just in case, I always sprinted from one end to the other, usually with Jools next to me. We stood in front of the telephone cubicle, a sturdy upright oak chair set behind a satin curtain held to one side with a gold cord.

'C'mon, let's go to the kitchen, Julie. Are you ready?' I'd ask, staring into the darkness.

'Okay, let's go.' And we flew down that corridor, eyes peeled and hearts pounding as we dashed to the sunny, yellow light at the other end. When my brothers were old enough, Mum let them have the car some Saturdays so they could go surfing, on the condition they dropped me off and picked me up from ballet. Later on we had a cream- and rust-coloured Holden and I had to sit in the back squashed between their mates. With the surfboards racked up, off we drove, looking for waves along the coast past Mona Vale, Warriewood, North Narrabeen, Collaroy, Dee Why and Manly. I felt most important and very privileged to be riding in the car with my brothers and their mates, even if they did pay me out all the while.

That's how each Saturday morning played out over the next ten years. I never missed class if I could help it. Most girls did netball of a Saturday morning; the buses were choked with the netball girls in their gaily coloured netball uniforms shrieking and laughing away. I was the odd one out on my way to ballet. During the week I attended a second class because I was an exam candidate, which meant leaving school early to catch a bus that would get me to class on time. My teachers often used this arrangement as a bargaining tool to get me to shut up. I was such a chatterbox.

'If you don't settle down and be quiet, Robyn Windshuttle,'

they would threaten, 'I will not let you leave early for your ballet class.'

It always worked; ballet was the most important aspect of my childhood. I especially loved the character work. The Swedish dance in Grade 1, the Tarantella, the Highland Fling; but my two favourite character dances were the Hungarian Czardas, and the Russian Dance depicting a peasant girl toiling the fields. My dad took me to see Rudolf Nureyev and Margot Fonteyn at the Capitol Theatre. This absolutely infuriated my Mum and caused bitter arguing between them. She wanted to go herself but Dad refused to take her. Afterwards, when she grilled me about the details of my evening at the ballet, I began to understand her indignation. Dad, the bastard, had taken his lover and used me as a decoy. He plopped me down in a dress circle seat and left me there alone while he watched the performance from somewhere else in the theatre, with his mistress.

Mum took me to see *Firebird* starring Lucette Aldous at Avalon pictures. Infused with the joy of dance I fell in love with *Swan Lake*, *The Red Shoes* with Moira Sheira, *Oklahoma*, the spectacular choreography of *West Side Story* and the quirky work of Bob Fosse in *Sweet Charity*. I wanted to be those dancers; I believed I could be those dancers. I danced around the house as if no one was watching, driving my father and my brothers mad with my endless energy.

'Sit down and keep bloody still!' they yelled.

Hazel had me skip Grade 3 and I went on to gain second place in the scholarships for Grades 4 and 5. The prize for that was an opportunity to attend holiday workshops at the prestigious studios of Scully Borovansky in the city. It was a long bus trip away but I never hesitated; this was where aspiring classical dancers studied full time and went on to professional careers with international companies, including the Australian Ballet. Entering that studio was like walking into another wonderful and exciting world altogether—the thud and creak of floorboards in the studios overhead; the piano accompaniment; the stern voices of Miss Potts and Miss Daintry; dancers scurrying to and fro. On one thrilling occasion I glimpsed Rudolf Nureyev making his way to a studio.

In time I took on extra jazz classes with Jan Chesire. Hazel didn't like that I was dancing at another studio, especially a contemporary, vibrant centre that made her jazz class seem boring. She interrogated me about my classes at Chesire's and demanded to know why I was not happy with what she was offering. I tried to avoid telling her because I knew my explanation would only enrage her but she wouldn't let it alone.

She kept on at me, determined to get a response, so in the end I told her. I blurted out the truth openly and honestly. 'Your jazz classes are boring.'

Well she nearly fell over with shock at my brazen honesty. 'Get to class,' she ordered. No one ever stood up to Hazel and as I scurried to the change rooms I couldn't quash a feeling of dread about my punishment for doing so. Her fury and wrath spilled over onto the studio floor where she stopped the class and vilified me in front of everyone. I stood there shaking and stunned, turning various shades of purple, enduring scorching humiliation. It was a horrible ordeal, a lonely and soul-destroying chastisement. The following week, Hazel installed Nancy Hayes, a prominent and much revered musical comedy star and a previous Meldrum's student, as head jazz teacher and I was banned from jazz class.

At home the demise of my parent's marriage was almost complete. My father's affair and my mother's anger fuelled their acrimony and tears. No one was listening to anyone; it was like a battlefield, every man for himself. Of an evening Mum got into the habit of waiting in the kitchen with the doors slightly ajar in anticipation of the uproar that was becoming a regular pattern in our lives. One night he stormed into the house after a hard day's work and a few beers. There was no hello, no how was your day, zero affection or interest in anyone about anything. He was hungry and cranky. He snarled at us 'Bloody lot of little parasites', flicking a tea towel at our limbs deliberately. It stung and burnt and he knew it. We darted about dodging him and then he sat down to eat. Like a barbarian he devoured that food in huge gulps, snorting and grunting, food dribbling down his chin. It always made me sick to watch. Then the unthinkable happened. The lid came off the salt container, spilling it all over his food. Absolutely charged with rage he stood up, screamed abuse at

Mum as if it was somehow her fault and he hurled the plate
of food at her. It flew through the air like an airborne missile,
narrowly missing her and smashing into the kitchen doors. By
the time it came to rest she had fled to Aunty Pat's house next
door, the smashed glass doors smeared and dripping in gravy,
meat and vegetables.

Dad finally left the family home when I was thirteen. Mum
eventually mustered the courage to file for divorce, which really
pissed him off. It probably should have been a sad time but it
wasn't. After years of conflict and strife, there was finally going
to be some peace. Dad bunked out at his beloved Palm Beach
Surf Club for a while and life went on. I think he loved his boat
crew more than he loved us.

4

$\mathcal{M}$y best friend, Joanna, lived a couple of streets behind me on Irrubel Road in a big house up a long driveway. Her house sat in a flourishing garden that backed onto a herb nursery. Jo and I met in kindergarten; we got on straight away. At Christmas I tagged along with her family to sing carols outside people's homes for charity and afterwards we drank lime cordial back at her house with all the other families in the balmy night air. In high school, Jo went off to a private girl's school while I attended Pittwater High, which had a dubious reputation because dope plants were found growing in the back paddock. The media had a field day with that and sullied the character of our beautiful Northern Beaches environment with sensationalist front-page headlines. Pittwater High became known as the druggie school for a while until the emergence of talented musicians, actors, athletes, models, surfers and performers transformed its image to one of an artistic and creative environment.

Jo and I grew together through our teens to the backdrop of 60s and 70s soundtracks: Joni Mitchell; Bob Dylan; The Doors; James Taylor; the Rolling Stones; the Eagles; Neil Young; Crosby, Stills and Nash; Seals and Croft; Carole King; Jimmy Page; Robert Plant; and The Beatles. We spent just about every weekend together. We were typical teenage girls trying to discover our identities. We sat up late into the night listening to music and talking endlessly about life, our dreams, our fears, boys and sex. Making that difficult journey through adolescence to young adulthood, we fought with our parents, defied them and at times despised them, but Jo and I always had each other, a support system when nothing made sense in the world. On weekends, we tanned our bodies in tiny bikinis at the beach and went to parties we were not supposed to go to. Mostly we stuck together when we went out but we had an arrangement that, should we separate during the night, we had to meet at the bottom of her long driveway when we got home. Whoever was there first had to wait for the other so we didn't have to explain to her oldies where we had been. I was usually the one to get there first, that is, until we got seriously busted by her father, Baz. He arrived home late one night—something we hadn't factored in—and as he turned into the driveway he caught me in the glare of his headlights attempting to hide myself in the bushes. He was absolutely furious and made me sit in their kitchen while we waited for Jo to turn up. When she finally showed we had to suffer one of his lectures. A glass of wine in hand, he blatted on while we sat in mock remorse. Later on in bed we giggled about the whole ordeal.

Usually on a Friday night Jo made her way around to my place to hang out. There wasn't a whole lot to do on the Peninsula for seventeen-year-olds but with such a colourful and large family there was always action at my place. We were an arty family, our humble house full of character. Everyone wanted to be at our place, and having older brothers was a drawcard for lots of my friends; I suspect the boys were the reason some of them came—the ones who were intrigued with brothers because they only had sisters. I never understood what they thought they were missing out on. Our household was crowded, noisy and aggressive with all that testosterone.

All the visitors became too much for Mum at times. She was glad we had friends but the constant presence of teenagers and the consumption of every skerrick of food drove her mad. My brothers played guitar in a band out the back in the old temporary dwelling, 'ye old dog house', and always after a jam session or after a surf they'd barge into the house, lord it all over us chicks, ordering us out while they raided the fridge, ate everything in sight and generally made a big mess, which we had to clean up. If it wasn't my brothers' mates eating everything, it would be Jo and me or my sisters and their best friends. Sitting up in bed late at night, head to toe, scoffing peanut butter and vegemite toast until Mum screamed from her bedroom to 'Get to bloody bed'. The one consolation for my mother was that no one liked her blue cheese, so no matter how many friends we had over or how empty the fridge, she knew her blue cheese and her Vita-Weats would remain untouched.

ಌ

I had my first joint on Mona Vale headland with Steve. He was a long-haired, bearded hippy guy, seven years older than me, and a bit of a local surfing legend back then. He competed at Bells Beach and other prominent surfing comps and I thought he was gorgeous, all the surfie chicks did. I was only fifteen and far too young for him but it was with Steve on a sunny afternoon, looking out over the Pacific Ocean all the way to Manly, that I first smoked grass. Pot was grown locally in the glasshouses at the back of Mona Vale long before the ghastly sprawl of suburbia took hold out there. Just about everyone I knew smoked dope; it was embedded in the surf culture of the Northern Beaches. We smoked Thai Buddha sticks, which came in tin-foil packages, or hash oil, which came in caps. Back then, smoking dope was considered light, harmless fun. We'd giggle a lot, get the munchies and cruise down to the beach.

My teenage years were idyllic; a wonderfully free and simple lifestyle; a time when we watched iconic surf films like *Morning of the Earth* and *Big Wednesday*. We got around in Kombi vans, smoked hooch and walked the track up to Barrenjoey Lighthouse.

At the beach we watched surfing legends like Nat Young, Terry Fitzgerald, Midget Farrelly and Bob McTavish. Shane Steadman opened one of the first surfboard factories in industrial Brookie and we got around in surf wear that 30 years later would become mainstream fashion. Pot was a part of that lifestyle. It intensified our sensitivity to light, music and movement, and it fuelled our imaginations and urged us to be creative and artistic. We questioned the conventional values of the establishment, adopted the new counterculture where we *dug* peace and freedom, described mind-blowing experiences as 'heavy' or 'unreal' and labelled conservatives as '*straight*'.

One hot summer afternoon Jo and I and a group of people from Mona Vale Beach went to see John Mayall in concert at the State Theatre. We all met at the beach, smoked a few whopping big joints and then took off in someone's Kombi into a pinkish dusk sky. By the time we made it to the city a throng of long-haired, bearded 'heads' and kurta-clad women were already congregated outside the theatre. Everyone was excited and edgy with anticipation. It was hot and sticky and the smell of sweaty bodies was acrid. We were standing there among the boisterous crowd in zombie mode when out of the corner of my eye I glimpsed Jo behaving strangely. Her head was bobbing back and forth and up and down like a puppet suspended on a string. The hue of her face went from grey to deathly white and it took a few seconds for me to realise she was about to faint. I freaked out, grabbed her and yelled for help.

One of the boys panicked, then said, 'Fuck! Quick, you guys, let's get her into the car.' She passed out into the boys' hands as they swiftly evacuated her from the scene and whisked her off to the Kombi two streets away, with me running alongside holding her hand.

By the time we had her laid out in the back of the Kombi she had come to. Because she hadn't eaten all day she'd totally spun out after the smoke. There is nothing worse than spinning out, it is the most ghastly feeling, like extreme sea sickness. The boys took off while I revived her with chocolates—Darrell Lea was close by—and, satisfied she was going to be alright, I left her there to recover. I wasn't going to miss John Mayall.

When I got back to the theatre, pandemonium had broken out. Some quick-witted person had called an ambulance for Jo and there were cops, sirens blaring, lights flashing, lots of pushing and shoving and general paranoia. Everyone was worried they were going to get busted. The cops weaved their way through the crowd stopping at random, asking questions. Ambulance officers searched for the girl who had fainted. All we could do was look on silently, observing the situation unfold. We kept our mouths shut and receded into the crowds, avoiding detection.

∞

At seventeen I met Gary at the beach. I had on a barely there red bikini, one that tied at the sides, when he came up to me outside the milk bar and said hello. He was Canadian and not like the local boys; he was a loner and an outsider. Gary had a handsome face and a strong surfer's body. The upper half of his otherwise perfect teeth were heavily stained from all the dope he smoked. He had long strawberry blond hair that he mostly wore in a ponytail and he always carried mineral salts and vitamins in a beaded hessian bag. Gary was vegetarian and passionate about preventative medicine and macrobiotics. He introduced me to brown rice, fresh juices and natural foods. He educated me about the value of unprocessed and unrefined produce.

Nowadays Gary's eating habits would be considered mainstream, but back then he was regarded as a bit of an eccentric. He took me to the first natural health food restaurants in Sydney, in Liverpool Street and at Bondi. We saw Elton John and Jethro Tull at the Hordern Pavilion and the Rolling Stones at Randwick Racecourse. Socialising with Gary's work colleagues and clients who lived in Double Bay, Rose Bay and Woollahra in the Eastern Suburbs of Sydney opened me up to life outside the 'Insular Peninsula'. His heavy dope smoking didn't bother me because that's what everyone did on the Peninsula. Gary shared a weatherboard beach house just beyond the sand hills over from Avalon Beach with his mate John. Jo and I spent a lot of time in that house, she with John and I with Gary. The house always had the nutty, earthy aroma of natural foods and incense and the kitchen bench was always cluttered and overflowing with mess left after a serious bout of the munchies. After smoking, we scoffed rye bread with raw peanut butter, sultanas and banana, strawberries and yoghurt or tempura and rice and then the boys would grab their boards and we'd duck through the back fence and over the dunes to the surf.

Gary worked for his brother at an import company bringing in goods from Asia and it was his job to drive up and down the coast selling the Indian and Balinese merchandise. His car was always stacked with kurtas, bags, skirts and T-shirts embroidered with mirrors; batiks; and chillums and all the other paraphernalia for dope smoking. Whenever I could, I took off with him. Back then Byron Shire, our favourite destination, was the most beautiful, lush countryside imaginable. The deserted beaches were pristine and isolated, the undulating hills sparsely populated. We stayed with friends in big old weatherboard houses with wide verandas and stone fireplaces or dined with his client, a woman from Double Bay in Sydney who owned the one and only chic boutique in the main street of Byron. We ate soy burgers at the sole health food restaurant up the road from the pub and we did the markets in Bangalow, which drew all the hippies out of the hills on weekends. We got around barefoot in sarongs, watched the sun rise and sniffed out the best waves up and down the eastern coast of Australia. It was an easy-going life for a while.

5

I stuck at ballet all through my teens. No matter what was going on socially, I rarely missed class. My pre-occupation with dance meant spending a lot of time on my own, which I thrived on. The word 'potential' was often tossed about and I felt confident in my ability so it was easy for me to visualise becoming professional. Dance had been the one constant, reliable source of joy for me; my whole identity had become wrapped up in it. When I was fourteen, my mother suggested that it was perhaps time to give it up but I couldn't imagine life without dance. Instead I contemplated full-time study while I worked my way up to Intermediate RAD. I extended my knowledge of contemporary classes with Karen Kerkhoven in her tiny studio in Newport and danced at the choreographic competition in her prize-winning ballet *Getting Clean*. It was Karen who suggested the contemporary studios of Bodenwieser would be just right for me if I decided to take the path of full-time study.

Each year hundreds of aspiring young dancers from across Australia, most of whom have undertaken years of lessons, audition for the Australian Ballet School. I loved classical ballet but as I grew into my teens I recognised that I wasn't going to cut it as a classical dancer in a mainstream company. I knew I had talent but I didn't have the petite frame—I was too tall. Besides, it would have required massive family support and I'd heard sad stories of talented dancers abandoning school early, of ballerinas succumbing to anorexia, of parents who had mortgaged their whole lives, of broken hearts and disillusionment, all of which turned me off. A classical path seemed out of the realms of reality and who was going to pay for all that anyway?.

Not my father, that's for sure. He scoffed at the notion of full-time study. Not that he knew anything about my life; since his separation from Mum, I'd hardly seen him. He had a new wife who was only six years older than me and he showed little interest in his kids' lives unless we did something that he could boast about to his cronies. He didn't know what I was up to, who my friends were or what I was feeling. I can't remember any meaningful interaction or affectionate embrace between us. Though there was the time I started pointe work and wanted so badly to show him how clever I was. He dropped by home one Sunday morning with two of his boat crew. He barged in, abused my mum just for being alive, picked up the oar or whatever it was he needed, then bolted. As he was reversing up the driveway I dashed out, calling to him frantically, 'Dad . . . Dad . . . look,' as I bourréed across the patio in my new pink satin toe shoes. They cheered and laughed loudly and smiled broadly but Dad's fleeting attention was wounding. I felt silly and embarrassed about being proud of myself and for wanting him to be proud of me too.

When I had told Dad I wanted to study full-time dance upon leaving school he harped on about having a second string to my bow and insisted I attend secretarial school. In retrospect it was good advice, but there was no sitting down and talking about my options—it was an order and if I didn't obey, I was a bloody idiot. Had he, or my mother for that matter, encouraged me on some other creative path or to at least finish my Higher School Certificate, perhaps even university, I may have been interested. I certainly had the academic ability and achieved well at school, but it didn't occur to either of them to push for something different from their own narrow experiences of youth. Their battler mentality prevented them seeing a different future for their kids. My mother pushed me into a job in a supermarket as a checkout girl. I hated the idea but she thought it was a great start. As it turned out I was hopeless, probably because of my bad attitude—I was ashamed to be a checkout girl and embarrassed when I ran into people I knew.

I tried secretarial school for a while and the arrangement was for me to live with my father at his trendy terrace in Kirribilli just up from the ferry on the foreshores of Sydney Harbour. The address was certainly favourable and handy to the school but I hated living with him and the woman he had overthrown his family for. I felt estranged and awkward. I didn't have the father–daughter connection that most other young women took for granted, this was not my home and I didn't want to be a secretary.

I endured the secretarial school for a few months but I had this sense I was in the wrong place. I enjoyed the shorthand because it was akin to learning a language and I was good at languages, but learning to type to music was hilarious; I was unable to take it seriously. I wanted to be in the dance studio and I knew if I was going to get anywhere with dance I had to do full-time study. Thousands of girls learn ballet and then take on casual classes as adults but it's full-time study that develops a dancer's talent. I tried to talk to Dad about that but he wasn't interested in what I felt or what I wanted. So I boldly stood up to him and flat out refused to continue with secretarial school. Predictably he exploded with rage and denigrated me for being foolish and obstinate in blatantly disobeying him.

'You're just like your mother,' he roared. I stood, unflinching, resolute and fearless while he hurled insults and abuse. When it was over—and with tears streaming down my cheeks—I packed up my things, walked out of his house, out of secretarial school and pretty much out of his life forever.

෴

A classical career might have been out of the question but contemporary, jazz and musical theatre were just as thrilling for me. The Bodenwieser Ballet was the first truly influential modern dance company in Australia and Margaret Chapple and Keith Bain were keeping the Bodenwieser spirit alive. I slogged it out every day and trained hard. I loved it. I kept up my classical training with occasional classes at Scully's, Halliday's and Valrene Tweedie's, which, like most studios, was tucked away up a dark alley in a decrepit old building. But I spent most of my time at the contemporary studios at Bodenwieser practising the techniques of Lester Horton and Martha Graham.

I was tutored by the best, including Graham Watson, who installed live jazz musicians in studio, Jaquie Caroll, Chrissie Koltai, Graham Murphy, Margaret Chapple, Ross Coleman and Peggy Watson. ABC television came to film what was regarded as the most avant-garde dance centre in Australia. I thrived in this fertile, stimulating atmosphere. I loved the studios, the mirrors, the hung floors, the hard work, the sweaty, tired body at the end of each day; I was exactly where I wanted to be. Full-time study as opposed to casual classes marks the difference between an average dancer and a good dancer. Studying everyday improves and builds up technique, versatility and style.

෴

It's tough trying to crack your first dance job. No one takes you seriously when you are inexperienced. You can work tirelessly in the studio day after day, wondering if you are ever going to be able to transfer all your hard work and commitment into a professional career, to move out of the studio and onto the stage in front of a paying audience. Then, out of the blue, an opportunity presents itself and you are on your way.

My first paying dance job was with a small-time entrepreneur who had a contract with Westfield. Terry Stewart produced shows as a promotional tool for the newly established Westfield shopping centres in Sydney, Adelaide and Melbourne.

I was sitting in the foyer at Bodenwieser's one unusually quiet afternoon, waiting for class. Kerrie Ridley, one of the other full-time students, was on reception that day and when the call came from Terry Stewart looking for a dancer, I don't think she even considered me. But then she glanced over and said suddenly, 'Robyn . . . Robyn will probably be interested.' I was just so excited to be offered professional work I jumped at the chance.

Terry's show was fun, easy and a great experience, and the travelling to Adelaide and Melbourne was a bonus. I'd always had a bristling curiosity about the experiences travel could deliver.

From an early age, and in some small measure, I had an innate sense that a bigger destiny awaited me. I felt excitement about life's possibilities beyond the confines of my life on the Peninsula and the turmoil at home. Perhaps such dreams were inspired by all those Hollywood musicals we watched as kids. Maybe it was just the pure joy of dance that sometimes I felt would burst right out of me that triggered my daydreams about dancing around the world to far-off lands. This first job was an opportunity to travel and to dance and get paid for it. I saw it as a launching pad to the new horizons and adventure I yearned for.

After the Westfield Shopping Centre gigs, Terry offered me a three-month contract with Chandris Line on board *Patris*, a Greek cruise ship. I would be part of the entertainment crew for the cabaret show each evening. We had a repertoire of ten different shows; my favourites were a Brazilian routine with electric green, pink and yellow tulle skirts; a clown show that worked well during bad weather from a tropical cyclone; some Louis Armstrong favourites; and a sharp jazz routine to the 'Theme from *Shaft*', which we performed in dark purple unitards.

Apart from the shows each night we had to glam up and assist hosting the occasional cocktail party, but during the day our time was our own and I had one of those shipboard romances you read about in corny novels. His name was Christos, a handsome Greek officer, who I often caught checking me out from a distance. We started to meet by the pool of a day and then each night he'd appear at the back of the auditorium during the show's finale. He'd saunter in and stand there grinning, watching me.

I came to look forward to his presence there and would be quite miffed if he didn't turn up. After the show we'd meet for a drink—never anything stronger than a juice for me—and steadily our friendship blossomed. It wasn't long before I got into the habit of sneaking up to his cabin in the officer's quarters where I'd lie with him, wrapped in his arms until the early hours of the morning. When the ship docked, he escorted me around the islands to sample local foods, see festivals and peruse the markets; I usually wore my unsophisticated hippy clothes, which he thought was very cute, while he looked quite handsome in his white officer's uniform. For three glorious months we cruised around Fiji, Vanuatu, New Zealand, Pago Pago and Tonga.

While I was away, Gary wrote me lots and lots of intense love letters in messy red pen, hoping to lure me back to him. I almost gave in and disembarked at one point. I even notified Terry and my mum of my intentions but I was having too much fun, and once I got home I realised I hadn't missed anything. My mum was relieved about that; she didn't want me giving up anything for Gary.

After the show one night I met a pot-smoking surfer guy in the disco who invited me to smoke a joint with him up next to the funnel. He reminded me of the guys back home so I agreed and went via the outer deck where a warm, salty wind blew hard in my face and a golden moon lit up the ocean. I remember the ship's creamy wake frothing about the stern under the spectacular night sky.

Standing next to that towering black funnel, I felt minute and insignificant. Strong gusts of wind tossed our hair about our faces and we had to huddle together to stop the joint from blowing out or burning too quickly. It was typical Aussie weed, bitter and dry, but it got us stoned alright, and with grins on our faces and that warm feeling coming over us, we began our descent back to the disco. Suddenly I was grabbed and ushered off so hastily it took me a few minutes to realise what was going on. We were busted. I had been apprehended by two uniformed men and was being whisked off to an interrogation room. I craned my neck to see what was happening to the long-haired hippy guy and saw he was being escorted in the other direction by several uniformed men. I was made to sit in the galley, stoned, under surveillance of the ship's purser and my boss, Terry, and supported by my friend Gail. They weren't angry with me, more irritated by the inconvenience of it all. The hippy guy was to be disembarked at the next port while I got off lightly with a harsh reprimand from Terry.

Towards the end of my contract, Christos startled me with a proposal of marriage. He wanted me to return to Greece with him as his young blonde wife. I was stunned and flattered but I had no intention of doing any such thing. We met once more in Sydney when his ship docked. He came bearing gifts—a silk kimono and a delicate silver watch—and over the years he kept in touch with postcards from all different parts of the world that he always signed, 'with fond affection from your Christos'.

6

*S*outh Sydney Junior Rugby League Club was one of the biggest clubs in Sydney back in 1973. In those days there was huge money for productions so it was very respectable work for dancers. The shows attracted stars from all over the world. I remember working with Al Martino, Tony Bennett, Frank Ifield, Lorna Luft, Kamahl, the Delltones, Little Pattie, Judy Stone . . . to name a few.

I auditioned for Ken Jeacle, the choreographer at Souths Juniors, telling myself it was only a temporary step. With all that full-time study behind me and some promising talent, I had aspirations to make it into a contemporary company some day but I had no plan in place nor did I have a clue how I was going to make that happen. I thought club work was glitzy and a bit tacky and the artifice of it all clashed with my idealist notions of living a down-to-earth, natural existence, but a dancer back then couldn't afford to be snobbish about work. There were mainstream classical ballet companies, musicals requiring a trained voice, or sports clubs. I was getting paid good money to dance and to perform in a respectable club. I decided it would do.

Souths Juniors had eight dancers in the ballet but with the coffers overflowing they wanted bigger and better productions. The auditorium was packed out every night with families and patrons who dined in the restaurants and used club facilities. We did two shows a night from Wednesday to Sunday. I was the youngest of all the girls and the most irreverent. I didn't take it too seriously and clowned around a lot.

Every now and then I came to work straight off the beach in my sarong, hitchhiking all the way from the Northern Beaches to Kingsford in the south. I'd fly through that auditorium, dash past Lionel, the musical director, warming up his orchestra, bolt through the glass doors to the dressing room and burst in to find all the girls shaking their heads in dismay, before getting into big trouble from the stage manager. Robyn Whelpton—she was Red Rob; I was Blonde Rob—good friend that she was, always covered for me, assuring everyone I'd be there and with her help I always managed to get made up, frocked up and on stage just in the nick of time.

The Merry Minstrel Show was one of the bigger productions at Souths Juniors. A couple of stars headlining the production had been flown out from London from the original musical to lead a chorus of singers, actors and dancers. After a six-week stint at Juniors it was going on tour through New South Wales and then on to New Zealand. I left Juniors at that point and decided to skip the New South Wales leg of the tour to trek with Gary and his cousin Lee in a big old purple bus instead. I'd been living with Gary for some time by then and I decided travelling up and down the coast selling Gary's merchandise and cruising in and out of coastal towns following the surf would be more fun.

My mother didn't approve of my relationship with Gary. Looking back now, I don't really blame her. He was a heavy dope smoker with an introverted personality and she wanted more for me. I knew I wouldn't settle for Gary but Mum and I began to fight about it. We began to fight about everything. During my middle school years we had been close; I had looked up to her all through my childhood and she'd relied on my competence and awarded me huge responsibility. I saw myself as her helping hand and I'd defended her to my father over and over again.

She was my ally, but somewhere in my late teens we came apart. We argued about everything; it was a constant battle of wits between us. I disliked her new boozy persona and her flamboyant appearance and she didn't like my newfound independence. I resented having to explain my actions to her all the time and was indignant about her intrusions into my privacy. She was tactless, insensitive and blunt and rarely listened or understood what I was on about.

When she did take the time to listen she was impatient and

dismissed my feelings as ridiculous. I despised her for that—it felt like betrayal. Since the horrific time with my father and their separation she'd been busy having a good time as a single woman. I get that now but at the time I saw her as selfish and shallow. We fought bitterly. Mum had always known how to take care of our needs as kids, but as our intellectual and emotional needs developed she was challenged and I resented that. My tough exterior and confidence led her to assume, ignorantly, that I was streetwise when really I was an emotionally immature teenager. No one escapes unscathed from the pain and fear of an abusive family environment. It was an exhausting, frustrating and mostly disappointing time. I hated our ugly exchanges, hated myself for the pain I was causing and hated her for not knowing how to deal with it.

When Gary had asked me to move in with him, I saw it as a way out of a tumultuous home life. 'I'm going to move in with Gary,' I announced as Mum swept the concrete patio. I'll never forget the pain that shot through me when she quietly acknowledged my decision without any fuss. She just kept on sweeping and didn't fight for me to stay. She made no attempt to warn me about the potential difficulties of moving in with Gary. I was ambushed by humiliation and hurt from somewhere deep and unknown to me. Out of shame I stood there struggling to hide my true feelings even though I was rocked to the core. After five kids and an abusive husband she was more than ready to set me free.

7

The Merry Minstrel Show had completed its months of touring around New South Wales and rehearsals were soon to begin for the New Zealand tour. My friend Red Rob mentioned that Ken Jeacle needed another dancer. My relationship with Gary was petering out by then, and the idea of travelling to New Zealand really excited me. In the beginning, living with Gary had been fun and easy. He cared for me more than I cared for him and I liked that; I trusted him. I enjoyed playing house and I was free of family conflict. But the sense of belonging and affection we shared had become stale. He was a very intense man, and he smoked too much dope, which made him moody and anti-social. He was often jealous of the attention my vibrant personality drew and that irritated me. I had outgrown him and was ready to move on in life so I called Ken about a place in tour.

Ken Jeacle was as pleased as punch to hear from me because I knew the choreography, I'd done the show at Souths Juniors, I fitted all the costumes and he could slot me in without any fuss. I was thrilled to bits and my mother was thrilled to bits for me. During the rehearsal period I moved back home. Despite the hurt and the pain we caused each other, we always managed to get over the difficulties and were able to pull together, for a while at least.

The tour would take us around the North and South Islands of New Zealand and we would perform in the charming old Queen Victoria theatres. Living, working and travelling with the same crew of people for weeks on end inevitably leads to a hierarchy establishing itself: a pecking order of management and performers from the stars of the show down through the ranks of dancers, musos, stage crew, costumiers and bus driver. The routine of hotel check-ins, rehearsals, dinners, performances and after-parties cocoons you from an external life. For the duration of the tour you become privy to the most personal and private details of perfect strangers whose lives become inextricably woven with each other's, like family. Everyone finds their possie, we get to know each other's moods and idiosyncrasies and we live with it. I carried a box of health food supplies around with me and Red Rob told me it annoyed everyone because I kept the bus waiting while I packed it up. Gary, the dance captain, had brought his family on tour, so we had to endure marital spats and bratty behaviour from his kids. Roy, the operatic tenor, had a roving eye for the dancers, especially Red Rob, which we paid him out heaps for, and Tony, the bass baritone, was argumentative, pedantic and disagreeable with everyone.

When the show closed in one theatre we'd pack everything up, load it all onto the bus and go off to do it all again in the next town at the next theatre. Upon our arrival in a new town we usually had a free night to settle into our accommodation before rehearsal the next morning. Some of the cast got together to play canasta, others relished their quiet time alone and I took this free time to bake hearty lamb dinners with herb-marinated vegetables for some of my closest buddies.

Inevitably I hooked up with Raymond. He had a wicked sense of humour and a sexy cute appeal. To break up the humdrum of coach travel, Raymond and I planned little trips outside the itinerary. We left the bus to make its way to the next town while we took off for a day or two in a hire car. In Queenstown, as the coach pulled out for Dunedin, we sped off over to Fiordland National Park. In Christchurch we rode hired bicycles against a biting chill to get to the theatre. By the time we arrived, our cheeks were a rosy flush and our bodies were all warmed up for the performance. We barbecued on the shores of crystal clear Lake Wakapitu, picnicked on the beaches in the Bay of Islands, went boating, swimming and surfing in Whangarei and Waitangi. In Rotorua, the heartland of Maori culture, we watched geysers thrust up from volcanic craters, gaped as bubbling mud baths spat and burped, and bathed naked in steamy hot springs. In Dunedin we bought fur coats in an op shop and somehow I managed to make the front page of the *Dunedin Star* in the form of a full-page, black-and-white photo inset captioned 'Cheeky Robyn'; a photographer had snuck back stage and secretly snapped a few photos, which infuriated management but served as a great promotional tool for the show.

The three-month tour whizzed past and, when the show finally closed in New Zealand, we flew back into a hectic schedule of performances in Australia.

☙

After *The Merry Minstrel Show* tour the world felt empty. I'd had a good taste of travel and that had made me restless. Life back home with my mother was mundane and the Peninsula seemed narrower than ever. I wanted to get overseas but wasn't quite sure how I was going to manage it. In the meantime Raymond was putting together some dancers and choreography for a show with Alf Garnett at Revesby Workers' so I jumped at the work as a means of filling in time while I hatched a plan.

Till Death Us Do Part was a hugely popular British sitcom in the seventies. I had never tuned into it and didn't get the humour until I saw the show live. Alf, alias Warren Mitchell, was absolutely hilarious and had the auditorium packed and the audience lying in the aisles with laughter every night with his particular brand of Cockney humour. Backstage he kept to himself until his fifteen-minute call, when we'd catch a glimpse of him emerging serenely from his dressing room, making his way quietly to the wings and then bursting out onto stage and into character to the resounding cheer of hearty applause. I couldn't help but notice his fit body and I could see under all the stage makeup that he had a handsome face. Apart from the odd glance from a distance and the briefest of encounters backstage, I can't recall any communication between Warren Mitchell and the dancers until one Sunday after a matinee.

The show had finished, I was on my way home and waiting for a bus with a couple of the other girls when this big black limo pulled up alongside the bus stop on busy Canterbury Road. We stood gobsmacked with surprise when the window opened and Warren Mitchell's face appeared. He looked at me and offered us a lift. I was embarrassed by his attention and felt silly explaining that my journey was a long one, all the way to the Northern Beaches. I was certain he wouldn't want to go that far out of his way but he insisted and wouldn't take no for an answer. I accepted the lift for at least part of the way and we all climbed into the back. The driver pulled out from the kerb and drove on.

There was silence for a few minutes and then from the front passenger seat, Warren turned around to face me. He was quite gorgeous, I remember, and I felt silly that I was in such a flutter.

'What is your name?'

'Robyn,' I replied. My girlfriends looked on silently.

'Would you care to join me for lunch. I'm only in Sydney for a few more days?'

I flushed with embarassment. I didn't really know what to say. He must have thought me a bit of a dingbat or very childish at the least. I looked back at his smooth, tanned face, his dark eyes, his elegant clothes and the slightest hint of a grin forming on his lips. Gosh, Warren Mitchell is asking me out and he is alright, I thought. I sat there in a dither for a few seconds and caught the driver's eye in the rear-view mirror. Then Warren spoke again in his refined accent.

'You are a most delightfully attractive young woman, you know. What's your telephone number?' he asked, taking out a pen from his jacket pocket.

I smiled self-consciously and couldn't find the words to say no, so I accepted his invitation but secretly tussled with the idea. I wanted to see him but I wondered why a man of his age and stature wanted to have lunch with the likes of a young unsophisticate like me. I worried he might find me boring and I didn't know what I was going to talk about with him.

His call came a few days later. Mum answered the phone, completely unaware it was Warren Mitchell.

'Phone for you, Robyn,' she called. 'Someone with a lovely voice.'

He'd done his homework, he explained, and suggested Jonah's at Whale Beach for lunch. But as I knew I would, I sheepishly turned him down. I hated squirming my way out of a date. I was still so inept at it and not completely certain of what I really wanted anyway. I could tell by the tone of his voice he was a little disappointed but he let it go with very gracious best wishes for my future. As soon as I hung up I had that dreadful feeling that perhaps I'd made the wrong choice.

My mother screamed with excitement when she discovered she had spoken to Warren Mitchell on the phone.

8

It is a hot Sunday morning at Newport Beach, one of those superb summer days so bright the glare is blinding. From where I'm lying up the northern end the crowd is just a mirage; a quivering scene in slow motion. I can hear the squeals of happy children having fun in the frothy white shallows close by. The peak, a popular surfing spot, is teeming with boogie boarders and surfers all vying for waves. Further out, the boat crew is in training, rowing in perfect rhythm up and back the length of the beach. I can hear the heave of the oarsmen as the sweep's voice pushes them harder and harder. Toddlers play with buckets and spades on the shore line, teenage girls show off their nubile bodies in skimpy bikinis while rotund older men and women lounge under colourful umbrellas. Between the flags sunseekers amass. Young, old, fat, thin, foreign, local, rich, poor: all beach lovers, sunworshippers.

I doze in and out of my blissful reverie contemplating the adventure I am about to embark upon. I'm twenty and in a few weeks I will be jetting off to Hong Kong. I have a six-month contract to dance at Miramar/Kingsland in Kowloon. My accommodation and airfares are provided, which is just as well because in all the world I have only eight dollars to my name. I am not worried about my lack of funds, as my excitement at travelling overseas—and getting paid to do what I love—has eclipsed and dulled the precariousness of that. This is my chance to see the world. I've been yearning for this for as long as I can remember and the opportunity has finally materialised. I am on my way and I am burning with excitement.

Apart from surviving the landing at Kai Tak Airport, which was notoriously dangerous and had to be carefully approached by very skilled pilots lest they miss the runway altogether and land in the sea, the first thing that hit me in Hong Kong was the stench and the humidity. It felt like walking into a bowl of thick soup and then having to wade through it. The pungent smell, which I got used to pretty quickly, was putrid, acrid enough to burn my nostrils. The city was crowded and dirty and busy, teeming with life. Laundry dangled, flapping in the wind on the verandas of rows and rows of cramped, dingy flats. Stray dogs roamed the streets; rotten food decomposed down little alleyways; and opium addicts, relics from an era when opium smoking was a fashionable pastime, wasted away on the streets as designer-clad tourists scurried by. Luxury hotel complexes full of important business people, gem traders and rag traders stood incongruously next to dilapidated accommodation for the disenfranchised. I worried that I wouldn't be able to live there. I wasn't used to such crowded living conditions, tainted water and heavy pollution; it was a major culture shock for me.

At first it was just the three of us: Bron, Dale and me. Bron had broken out from a stable secretarial job for this gig and Dale, who was a good ten years older than us, had left her kids behind with her ex-husband and was on a quest to meet a wealthy guy. Red Rob and Julie Tanner arrived three months later and we all lived in a roomy top-floor apartment in Tin Man Toi Doh, Observatory Road, Kowloon, in Tsim Sha Tsui district. Dale got shitty about the mess Bron and I left in the kitchen and every now and then we raided her bedside table for where she kept her expensive luxury chocolates; that really pissed her off but we just thought that funny. My balcony and the rooftop, where we got together to do class every now and then, took in the panorama of Victoria Harbour throbbing with the energy of traditional Chinese junks, cargo ships and leisure craft across to Hong Kong and Victoria Peak. The Miramar Hotel complex was a five-minute walk away, down a narrow alleyway that snaked its way past shabby, ramshackle flats whose living rooms blared with the high-pitched tone of Chinese opera. You could hear and see right into people's crowded living spaces adjacent to open-air kitchens where fowl for Peking duck at local restaurants hung drying.

From our place we took a shortcut to Nathan Road and the Star Ferry through a dark labyrinth of laneways choked with food stalls, merchants flogging their wares, makeshift restaurants and busy canteens serving up hot, steamy dishes. At dawn, the only quiet time in Hong Kong, the streets would silently come alive with pyjama-clad tai chi devotees going through the graceful moves of their ancient, meditative art form.

Rehearsals started promptly after I arrived and the show was underway in no time. Bunny, our choreographer, swanned around in his kimono and lived in an apartment adjacent to ours where he sewed our costumes. Not long into our contracts he pegged me to do a solo bit for which a dazzling new costume was needed, so there was much fussing over fittings and sequins, measurements and choreography.

We had two shows a night, the second one at the sister club of Miramar across the harbour on Hong Kong Island to which we were ferried on a shuttle bus through a heavily polluted underwater harbour tunnel. We had an amah, Ah Fook, who kept our apartment clean and provided us with herbal remedies when we were sick and whose welcoming gift of tropical fish spawned millions of babies in our fish tank.

Dee was the mannequin of the show, which pretty much meant she just paraded around on stage looking glamorous. She was the darling of Hong Kong, a born and bred local, acquainted with everyone, and she knew just about everything happening in town at any given moment. She was the cool chick, with a million-dollar smile and slight American accent. After the show each night, Bron, Dee and I descended the stairs to The Scene, a disco in the basement of the Peninsula Hotel. We went to all the nightclubs in the big hotel complexes but The Scene was our favourite. I loved the energy of that place and the excitement and diversity of people on parade. Dave, a long-time Aussie expat, managed the nightclub and always greeted us enthusiastically. He kept a close eye on us while we hustled and grooved away in our flares and platform shoes, burning off our excess youthful energy until the early hours of the morning.

One night, a local film director chose the club to feature in some scenes for his latest movie. As usual I was boogying on down with Chris, a very beautiful Filipino gay boy who couldn't resist hanging around western dancers. 'The Hustle' was playing and we were going for it. I was still in full stage makeup and the dance floor was packed with hot and sweaty bodies when the director approached and invited Chris and me to stay on after closing to be part of the shoot. Wow! To get noticed on the dance floor and then invited to be a part of a film—how exciting! I quickly got the okay from the director to invite my friends into the shoot. We had so much fun.

I never got to see the film—I was long gone by the time it was released—but my friend Bron saw it and, years later, told me how hilarious it was, watching us hustling away on that dance floor;

especially the bit where I had to walk off set to remove my false eyelashes because it was so hot and steamy they were falling off.

∽

Dee, Bron and I were inseparable; we did everything together and looked out for each other. We were young and frisky and bonded by an idealism about life and love. In the crazy artifice and fast pace of Hong Kong, our camaraderie sustained us and kept us grounded. We decided to celebrate New Year's Eve by spending the night on the beach together. We wanted to see the first rays of early morning sun usher in the New Year. A close friend of Dee's—a patriarchal, debonair type and boss of a big department store in Hong Kong—picked us up after work, drove us to Big Wave Bay in his sleek Jaguar and left us there with some blankets to return to his festivities, reassuring us he'd be back to pick us up in the morning. Dee and I blew a joint—she always seemed to have a stash on her—and then we rugged up, huddled together and waited, trying to stave off sleep. We sat there in silence in awe of the magical night sky, surrounded by darkness with only the sound of waves curling onto the shore.

I don't remember falling asleep but when I woke I was so disappointed I'd missed the big moment. I scrambled to the top of a big boulder to witness an enormous golden ball of fire creeping up over the horizon. Dee and Bron remained asleep while I perched atop the rocks, mesmerised by the orange glow of the early morning sun.

Sometimes we ferried over to Lantau Island for the day and Dee showed us cheap restaurants that served the best of local Cantonese cuisine and were always crowded with noisy locals clustered around laminex tables. We did the tourist trail stuff: the Tiger Balm Gardens and Victoria Peak and we took high tea in the Peninsula Hotel. We had our shoes handmade and I had the tailor down the road make me a midnight-blue silk cheongsam. I loved the elegance and simplicity of that dress. We shopped in big hotel complexes and at congested markets but our favourite place was Shek O Village, the furthest point from the city.

Shek O is an ancient traditional Chinese community nestled around a small surfing beach. Clucking fowl and geese roamed freely up narrow laneways leading to vegetable gardens and a tea house where old ladies played mahjong and old men with thinning grey beards played chess. Tucked away behind bushes and electric fences in the surrounding hills, wealthy landlords lived in palatial homes with tennis courts and swimming pools. Shek O was slow-paced and tranquil and as often as we could we made the trek out to escape the hemmed-in feeling of the city.

Some months into my contract with Miramar, a friend of mine from way back, Jenny Ludeke, the girl who took the Grade 1 scholarship over me all those years ago, arrived in Hong Kong. She was touring with Disney on Parade and made a point of coming to see us all at our apartment. She had news for me.

'Rob, listen here!' she demanded, leading me away from the

others. 'The Bluebells over at the Palace are looking for a dancer. Why don't you audition?'

My heart leapt and my mind raced at this absolute cracker bit of information. The Bluebells were classically trained dancers who were too tall for mainstream companies. They had a reputation as the most beautiful leggy dancers who graced the stages of the famous Lido on the Champs-Élysées in Paris; the Casino in Beirut before it was bombed; Reno, Nevada; Estoril, Portugal; and the Palace Theatre in Hong Kong. The opportunity felt as though it had winged in from the heavens itself. I was exultant and nervous all at once. The Bluebell Girls were tall, really tall, and beautiful and I worried I wouldn't make the height.

'I'm not tall enough, Jen.'

'Then cheat. I know these guys, Rob. We'll work something out,' she reassured me. Her confidence and certainty was a bit enthusiastic, I thought, but I realised immediately she was right. How many times had I heard my mother say, 'Opportunity knocks but once, Robyn'? I had to give it a shot. I knew I had nothing to lose but still the butterflies and vague insecurities niggled in my head.

'Rob, for goodness' sake!' Jenny said. 'You are classically trained, you dance well and you have the long, slim figure they are looking for. Go on, you can do it. We just have to find a way of getting around the height thing.'

Becoming a Bluebell would mean new challenges and new and exciting destinations with an international company. My comfort zone would be upset for sure. My life would take off in another direction; I would travel further and further from home, and that scared me a little. I wasn't sure I was ready for such a big step. I argued with myself, searching for a definite yes. I was always after change, seeking it out when things got mundane. Boredom was my enemy; I knew that about myself even though I was still young. So, despite some lingering uncertainty, I made my mind up and organised an audition immediately. I would work the height thing out somehow and, as for my contract with Miramar, well there had to be away around that. I enlisted Dee's help to find a local solicitor to look over my contract with Miramar/Kingsland to see if there was any way to get out of it. It was only a matter of minutes before the solicitor informed me that my contract clearly stated the terms of my employment were on a weekly basis, and therefore I was only required to give one week's notice. I couldn't believe my luck.

Before the actual audition I had to meet Miss Bluebell herself backstage at the Palace, which was located on the third floor of The Excelsior Hotel in Causeway Bay. I wore an apple green full skirt with an emerald green velvet jacket and I had done my hair in a French roll to give me added height and glam effect. I was nervous, excited, eager and optimistic all at once but this meeting was only for her to approve of my appearance; there would be an audition with Bernard, the dance captain and choreographer, if she liked me.

Madame Bluebell was waiting for me about halfway down the dressing room, a long corridor with spectacular, extravagant-looking costumes hanging on one side and floor-to-ceiling mirrors on the other.

Bluebell stood with her hands clasped, looking very stern. She was quite elderly and immaculately dressed and the first thing she did was look me up and down. There was no smile nor any display of warmth; she just gave me the once over. After a few moments she began to question me. Why did I want to be a Bluebell? Did I know the reputation I had to uphold if I was given the job? Did I know the history of the Bluebells and did I understand how prestigious it was to become a Bluebell?

As I responded, she watched my every move, her piercing blue eyes (from which she derived her title) scrutinising my face, presumably summing up my appeal. After a long, nerve-wracking ten minutes, her demeanour softened and she said, 'Very good, dear. Be on stage tomorrow morning promptly at ten o'clock. Bernard will audition you.'

I thanked her for her time and dashed off, relieved. Outside it was cold and dark. A light rain had the streets glimmering in the glare and flash of neon lights. I darted for the Star Ferry, dodging the usual bustle of cars, buses, bicycles and pedestrians in a hurry to get to work on time back in Kowloon.

๏๏

Bernard had a reputation for being a surly Frenchman and a tough bastard, so I was a bit nervous about fronting up for a private audition. I was taking a long shot with an internationally renowned troupe who performed all over the world and, as a simple beach chick from Newport, two centimetres short of the required height, I felt slightly daunted. Whenever I felt nervous like that, or when feelings of inadequacy threatened to sabotage my endeavours, I adopted my tried-and-true philosophical approach, telling myself, 'What have you got to lose? Best to aim high and get somewhere close than never to aim at all.' So I marched boldly into the Palace Theatre with an honest and open heart, a positive attitude and an agreement with myself that, whatever the outcome, I couldn't lose.

Bernard was not as tall as I expected. He had an athletic build, a balding scalp and an almost good-looking face despite deep lines and a cold expression. He spoke English well enough but had a heavy French accent. He explained to me that the standard of work was very high and that most girls weren't successful because they were just not good enough. He was cocky and condescending; his dismissive manner was intended to make me feel I was nothing but an inconvenience to him. This did not deter me at all; in fact it had the opposite effect. I knew immediately that I had to shake off any nerves. This guy was hoping I would buckle and no way was I letting him do that to me. The feisty determination learned in my family paid off at times.

He shuffled around, fussing with the music for a few minutes, dragging his feet, before showing me a combination of steps. I followed his lead and took it all in. I walked it out, expecting to run it through with the music a couple of times but then he said, 'Okay, let's see it.' He hadn't given me any time at all. He was deliberately making it difficult for me but I didn't flinch. He stepped back and lit a cigarette, dragged on it heavily, then exhaled slowly. His menacing attitude gave me the distinct impression he had written me off before I'd even started. But I knew that I was going to get this audition, even if he didn't. So I went for it.

I executed his choreography with style, presence and perfect timing. I threw my high kicks with precision and grace, I walked elegantly and I danced confidently. When I was finished he said nothing for a few moments but I knew I had him. I could see and feel he was pleasantly surprised even though he refused to acknowledge it openly. A sense of triumph surged within me as I stood there catching my breath.

'Okay, okay, how tall are you?' he demanded.

'I don't know, about one-eighty-five, one-ninety,' I lied.

'Well, you don't look tall enough,' he snapped. 'Come back in two hours to have a height test with all the other girls,' he barked, flapping his hands at me to leave the room. The whole audition had passed without the slightest hint of a smile from him.

I went back in two hours. The whole troupe was there waiting for me: a long chorus line of girls and boys from all over the world, and they were all exceedingly good looking and very tall. For the first time ever, I felt like a midget. As I arrived, all the dancers greeted me with friendly, warm smiles and two English girls, Maxine and Cindy, fussed over me like I was their long lost sister. They were ready to do anything to get me the job, so someone made the call seconds before Bernard turned up. We all had our rehearsal gear on, which was mostly long, flared, black jazz pants. The girls had to walk on stage in a long line with me in the middle to see if I measured up. What Bernard was not aware of was that all the girls bent their knees slightly, which you couldn't see because of the long flare in the jazz pants, and I stood on my tiptoe, which you also couldn't see because of the length of the jazz pants. After a few moments of scrutiny he gave me the nod, told me to turn up for rehearsals the following week then turned his back and walked off.

I was so happy. I could hardly believe I was in! There was rowdy applause and hugs from all the dancers and as everyone dispersed I was introduced to James, a tall, blond Aussie surfer type, one of two male leads and my roommate.

Bunny, my choreographer, and Michael, my boss at Miramar/ Kingsland, were horrified when I resigned, showing them the monumental flaw in my contract. They set about rectifying the other dancers' contracts immediately. They were disappointed and angry that I was deserting and hoped I would reconsider. When I refused they got shitty, which I didn't think was fair. I did feel some pangs of guilt about letting them down but I wasn't going to let this opportunity slip by, it was too good. The Bluebells' international reputation was far superior to Miramar and a contract with them would present opportunities for me to live and work in Europe. I had to jump.

My opening night at the Palace was thrilling. Rehearsals had been long and demanding and costume fittings tedious and frustrating, but now the curtain was going up. The orchestra began and I stood tall, held my head high and smiled. We floated down a staircase dressed in long, heavily beaded velvet capes lined with bright orange satin in front of an audience of hundreds. The stage was a mesmerising scene of colour, movement and luxury fabrics. The exhilarating roar of applause rose as we threw high kicks and struck elegant poses while the principals took centre stage and were lifted by their partners.

The Bluebells occupied the seventeenth floor of the Excelsior Hotel. James and I shared our room with a pond of turtles and my juice extractor so it always smelled of fruit and vegetable pulp and turtle poop. We put the beds together to make more room. Not that James stayed in very much. He was always gallivanting around, ever popular with so many men, both gay and straight. He had a good heart and was always on the lookout for true love. He joked that women were 'too bloody needy' and 'too much hard work'. He'd grown up in a conservative country town in an era when homosexuality was thought to be some kind of a disease. James was always the life of the party, independent, personable, confident and talented but I knew he carried scars deep inside.

I could see the pain as his eyes brimmed with tears when he spoke wistfully of his past.

James, along with the other Australian male principal, Michael, the female lead from Tasmania, and the star of the show, Liz, an English girl who went on to star in Vegas and Reno, became my new best friends. I hung out with them if I wasn't at Shek O or with my mates from Kowloon. Maxine and Cindy, English girls touring the world with the Bluebells, shared the room adjacent to mine. Their exquisite beauty and girlish charm had me thinking butter wouldn't melt in their mouth, so I was absolutely floored when they invited me to watch porn in their room and when they offered James and me acid trips. Then there was Ruud Vermeij, from Breda, Holland, who was hilarious and had a black sense of humour. We got to know each other waiting in the wings before curtain each evening. Hovering there in the reflecting glow of stage lights all glammed up in costume, we forged a friendship that would endure for many years to come.

Bernard was always cranky, and rehearsals were held up screaming matches and ugly confrontations between him and Liz about the timing—usually nothing more than a clash of egos. We performed two shows a night and a matinee on Saturdays. Each night James introduced the show to the international audience while dangling from a rope, miming to a Mandarin version of a welcoming spiel. Then Michael did the same in American-accented English. Each night brought a new wave of tourists, a full house every time.

Sometimes before the show a few of us smoked a joint in our room before going down for 45-minute call. We were so blasé about it all; getting stoned and then taking the lift to the third floor dressing rooms in fits of giggles. We had to negotiate our way around the stage, up and down elaborate stairs, weaving in and out of dancers, stage sets and intricate costumes in full stage makeup whacked off our faces. I don't know what we were thinking or how we managed it.

๑๑

After eight months in Hong Kong I'd had enough of the place. The routine of the show each night at the Palace soon became mundane compared to the exhilaration of my first night and I became claustrophobic within the geographical confines of Hong Kong. I'd had lots of lovers over the months and had been chaperoned all over Hong Kong, including a chauffeur-driven day trip up to the New Territories, which were just beginning to open up. But my romantic liaisons were mostly unremarkable little affairs, because everyone was always on the move. The transient nature of the tourists and business people was not conducive to forming meaningful relationships and I became very aware of how men could be so easily mastered by their lust; I was left feeling empty and lonely and I yearned for a more genuine connection.

My contract with the Bluebells was coming to a close too, so I had to think about where I was going—there was nothing to draw me back home. My mother had come over for a visit for my twenty-first birthday but it had been unpleasant. I was really excited about seeing her but from the moment she arrived she was dismissive, insulting and rude. She wasn't impressed with the state of my hotel room, what I wore or how I wore it or who I was seeing. I tried to be tolerant but I just couldn't manage and instead got annoyed and bitchy. Like me, my mother was disappointed that our mother–daughter catch up had not met her expectations but she became sulky and wanted to go home. To add insult to injury, she embarrassed me with her boozy, loud behaviour in the audience when she watched the show. It didn't go unnoticed by other cast members; everyone on stage could hear her and they all thought she was hilarious but I resented her inappropriate antics.

There seemed no point in me going home so I decided Europe would be the go. I sidestepped Bernard and wrote to Bluebell personally, asking for a place in Europe somewhere. I didn't ask for the Lido; I wasn't sufficiently hungry for that sort of prestige, nor would I appreciate it and I assumed that my height would rule me out for Paris. So, rather than be turned down, I didn't even ask. Bluebell replied promptly with an offer of a lead spot, which meant I'd have to be a nude, for the summer season in the Casino Estoril, Portugal. I was a bit nervous about becoming a nude, mostly because I had tiny boobs. Although I had an appealing figure I'd been self-conscious about my skinny chest since puberty. My mother had very generous bosoms and my sisters had buxom breasts too so I always felt I had missed out. Still I had done lots of topless sunbathing before so I told myself that this was no different. If you wanted to be a lead it was obligatory to be a nude. Besides which the nudes are always draped in such finery it's hardly a display of vulgarity. There would be four weeks' rehearsal in Paris and it was a smaller production for a more intimate cabaret room but I loved the idea of a coastal destination for the European summer.

Bernard was furious with me for going over his head and writing directly to Bluebell. In front of the whole cast he punished me mercilessly for not consulting him first. I had no idea it would cause so much animosity and I turned various shades of red and purple while he humiliated me. I felt so diminished and ridiculous but heartened when the troupe rushed to my side with encouragement and support. I now couldn't think of anything worse than continuing my employ under Bernard's direction and since I was desperate for a break from the artifice of city life, the south western tip of the continent sounded ideal to me.

Before I left for Europe I attended the big glamour event of that year: an international ready-to-wear fashion event hosted by the Excelsior Hotel at the Palace Theatre. The hotel was swamped with models, photographers, buyers and designers from all over the world. The place was jumping. Anybody who was anybody was there, all clad in haute couture, all trying to outclass each other. This was an invitation-only event but I befriended one of the models while she was getting her hair done for the show and she gave me a free pass. It was my first glimpse of supermodels on a catwalk previewing the upcoming fashions and oozing with glamour and elegance.

At the after-party, while mingling with the upper crust, I met Jenny, a very posh British-Sri Lankan girl about my age. She dressed exceedingly well, adorned herself with expensive jewellery and spoke with a refined British accent. She lived in Paris, studied at la Sorbonne in Paris and was holidaying in Hong Kong, staying in a large estate out at Shek O. I assumed she was wealthy and apparently well connected by the way she interacted so graciously with her acquaintances in the room that night. When she discovered I was on my way to Paris she surprised me with a hearty smile and a genuine offer of hospitality. She told me, very nonchalantly, that she had an apartment in Paris and her boyfriend, Diego, was there.

'Call him when you get to Paris. He will look after you,' she said, handing me the contact details. Then she invited me to her residence at Shek O to play a game of tennis before my departure.

I never made it for a game of tennis; I wasn't much of a tennis player and I thought I might embarrass myself socially, so I backed out. I was grateful for the contact in Paris though and decided to make use of it.

9

*M*y very first day in Paris, I met Daniel, a tall, handsome, charismatic Colombian man ten years older than me. He told me he was a photographer for the Nikon Gallery and he had an impressive camera as evidence.

From Hong Kong I'd flown to London and stayed with friends of Liz's in St John's Wood, just up from Abbey Road, which I thought was very cool, then I flew across the Channel to Amsterdam for a few days. James had organised for me to stay with friends of his, a married couple who met me at Schiphol Airport. From Amsterdam it's a five-hour train journey to Gare du Nord in Paris and I recall feeling really anxious to be finally pulling into the station; I was carrying a little block of hash hidden in my blush container and wasn't looking forward to having to negotiate my way to the accommodation Bluebell had arranged in the seventh arrondissement.

At the entrance of the modest bed and breakfast–style hotel, an irritated man with a woolly moustache and a white apron greeted me.

'Bonjour, *mademoiselle, bonjour,*' he sighed. '*Entrer, entrer s'il vous plait.*' He led me hurriedly up the stairs to my room before disappearing just as quickly.

None of the other dancers had arrived yet and, with three days before rehearsals, I was eager to make the most of my time. As soon as I'd settled into my room, I flew down the stairs, phoned Jenny's boyfriend, Diego, and dashed off to hail a cab to take me to his apartment in Rue Mouffetard.

I'd spent my childhood dreaming of foreign lands and big adventures; of escaping the trappings of day-to-day suburban life. I yearned for something bigger than the simple beach culture of my youth. I fantasised about passionate love, dancing around the world in exotic destinations, immersing myself in new cultures. There seemed to be no inoculation against my excitement for life's possibilities and my determination to discover the brilliant mysteries of life. I fretted and stressed about how it might happen but here I was, in Paris, City of Light, city of romance, land of the chic and cultured. It was absolutely stunning, all abloom with spring. I never imagined a city could be quite so breathtaking. As the cabbie weaved his way through congested streets and crazy drivers who all seemed to be oblivious of each other, I sat close to the open window and let the warm breeze brush over my face. We passed the Eiffel Tower, and negotiated our way around l'Etoile. We whizzed down tree-lined boulevards and avenues, past rows and rows of busy sidewalk cafés and over the Seine across beautiful Pont Neuf to Rive Gauche. I hadn't realised Rue Mouffetard was on the other side of the city and my driver must have known this and deliberately taken me by the longest route possible. I'd only ever read about all these famous landmarks and heard about the romance and beauty of this city so to be actually among it all was thrilling for me. I wanted to reach out and touch someone, jump for joy, shout out to the world how great this was for me. My excitement went into overdrive. I thought of my humble house in Newport on the other side of the planet and wondered momentarily what everyone was doing or if anyone was thinking of me.

The cab continued past gardens and parks and low-rise lime-stone buildings with terracotta chimney pots. I was so eager to get amongst it all and began by practising a bit of my schoolgirl French on the driver, who totally ignored me. I learnt quickly that if you are not French, the Parisians pretend they don't understand you, even though you know they do.

I left the cab just near le Panthéon and continued on foot a little farther to Rue Mouffetard, an enchanting cobblestone laneway lined with centuries-old buildings standing lopsided and supported by wooden and steel beams. I strolled past bars, cafés, boulangeries, épiceries, apartments and restaurants and un tabac, where old men with berets and thick moustaches sat drinking absinthe and smoking Gitanes. I was captivated by the ambience and pondered the Bohemian lifestyle of the past. I could almost see and hear the intellectuals, the painters, musicians and artists who had historically flocked to this part of the world in search of artistic freedom and expression.

I wandered along, eventually making my way up to Jenny's third-floor apartment in a lift that had wrought-iron doors whose clang reverberated through the whole building as they shut. Before I even had a chance to ring the bell the door flew open and I was ushered in and hugged and kissed so many times I felt like royalty.

As they led me inside I could hear in the background the haunting chant of thousands of soccer fans blaring from the television. A World Cup game was playing out. Diego, a short man with a basin-shaped head and a big C-shaped scar on his cheek, introduced himself first. He had a lisp and spoke like the Speedy Gonzalez cartoon character. Diego introduced me to the others. A well-spoken, well-dressed English guy, Ethan, who appeared to be the most cultured but turned out to be bland and boring. Zac, a nuggety African-American man who coincidentally happened to be a dancer and choreographer, sat arm in arm with his girlfriend, Amelie. Daniel was tall and lanky, unusual for Colombians, I would soon learn. His dominating presence struck me immediately. The moment I set eyes on him I sensed, if only fleetingly, that I should be wary of him. I couldn't help noticing his radiant smile but his strong face and intimidating glare scared me a little. He looked dishevelled, with a two-day growth and his shirt tails hanging out of his jeans.

I had their undivided attention, as if meeting an Australian was akin to meeting an alien. We spoke about the soccer, Australian sport and what had brought me to Paris. Jenny's apartment was modestly furnished and small, but cosy with a poster of the Rolling Stones on the living room wall. After a while I felt at ease enough to pull out the bit of hash I'd carried from Holland.

'Does anyone want a smoke?'

There was dead silence for about ten seconds until someone piped up. 'We've got something better than that, try this.'

A mirror with lines of white powder and a tube of rolled-up paper was offered to me. I had no idea what the powder was or what I was supposed to do with it. I thought it might be smack so I refused. They laughed at that and then reassured me that it wasn't heroin, it was safe—'This is *perico*, cocaine, baby, cocaine.' I hadn't heard much about cocaine other than it was used a lot by high society in the roaring twenties and that it had been an ingredient in the original Coca-Cola. Now I knew, through my new Colombian friends, that the South American Indians chewed coca leaves to relieve altitude sickness and to keep them alert at night while guarding their communities. Even though I was hesitant and worried that I was doing something really stupid, I took the tube anyway. I leant over and took my first line of cocaine, ignoring that little voice in my head telling me I shouldn't be doing this. I hardly knew these people; trusting them went against every instinct in my being.

Turns out I not only survived the experimentation but felt comfortable enough to park myself. I ended up staying with them for the next three days. Daniel waited on me hand and foot; they all did. Their attention was overwhelming and their charming manner disarming but it was with Daniel I felt a magnetic pull. It never occurred to me the camaraderie and social ease were the effects of the cocaine. Common sense should have alerted me that such warm feelings from perfect strangers were not normal. In comparison to the mind-numbing stone of weed cocaine was almost imperceptible and I thought it was boring in comparison. I announced this discovery and everyone in the room found it amusing.

∞

Of a morning, Rue Mouffetard transformed into a market place; a bustling bazaar, a scene reminiscent of a medieval setting with the cry of merchants selling their wares and people jostling for the best from an abundance of fresh produce on display. Vendors flogged their cheeses, wine, poultry, fish and seasonal fruits and vegetables, all open air, all fresh. Boucheries displayed whole pigs, offal and sides of meat and la boucherie chevaline, identified by the horse head over its entrance, supplied horse's meat. The smell of freshly baked baguettes and pastries tantalised passersby, crowded cafés overflowed onto the pavements, and street performers entertained.

After dinner we did cocaine. A pile of fine white powder was emptied onto a mirror, then it was diced into a finer consistency with a razor blade and then into individual lines that we sniffed through a rolled-up American bill. It gave a fresh, sharp zing that made my mouth and throat numb. Cocaine, I discovered, gives you a subtle high, zapping you into a heightened alertness. It was a party drug, a social enhancer. Conversation flowed effortlessly, time passed easily.

Sunday night arrived too quickly. I had to get back to the hotel to prepare for rehearsals the next morning and I needed a good night's sleep. I gathered my things together and said my goodbyes to my new friends and it was Daniel who escorted me to a cab and paid for my fare. Winding back across town I thought about the task ahead. I was about to start a new job and soon I would be on my way to Portugal. I was looking forward to the new choreography, new music, new friends, and I was eager to throw myself into it.

It was dark by the time I arrived; the foyer was dead quiet and dimly lit. I snuck in quietly, hoping not to wake anyone. Just as I began to climb the stairs a voice shot out at me from the shadows across the room.

'Robyn, is that you? I don't believe it!' And then I heard a cackle. I looked closer, squinting to make out who it was as he walked into the light and to my absolute surprise and delight I saw Ruud Vermeij, my Dutch friend from the Palace Theatre in Hong Kong.

Apparently Ruud had been waiting patiently for the missing Bluebell to return—without knowing it was me who would turn up. His anticipation turned to exasperation when she didn't show. Now that I was finally here it all made sense to him.

'Who else but you, Robyn, would turn up alone in Paris for the first time and disappear for three days without a word to anyone?'

The next morning we got stuck into rehearsals after an underwhelming breakfast provided for us at the hotel. I didn't drink coffee and I didn't know how I was going to get through the day on baguette and jam. The rehearsal studio was a five-minute walk away and decked out with hung timber floors, mirrors, an old piano and a tinny sound system. From the long windows—which we had fully open because it was so hot—we could see the iconic Moulin Rouge windmill up the road in Pigalle. I rehearsed in a pair of knee-high purple leather boots and by the end of the day my leotard was soaked with the bittersweet smell of sweat. We worked hard and long, perfecting our routines.

Once we had the choreography down pat we wore our glamorous headdresses to get used to them and I had to practise the fast costume changes along with the other lead. Most of the other dancers were English, including the other lead dancer, who had worked for Bluebell for years and had her own apartment in Paris. Bluebell had selected Corey, an American boy, to be dance captain and day by day the show slowly came together.

We put in hours of demanding physical work and were exhausted at night but I always had reserves of energy for Daniel. During those few weeks in Paris we gravitated towards each other steadily and unavoidably. His affection for me was seductive and alluring. His optimistic attitude appealed to me right away. He seemed intelligent and logical with a heart as open as mine and he understood the essence of who I was. We got on so well it was easy to let myself go and trust him. He was romantic, aggressively sexy, direct, at times tactless, but always adoring. I didn't recognise him as being bad for me at all.

Alarms should have gone off one day, though, when a pretty blonde woman appeared at the doorway. Daniel and I were snoozing side by side, naked in his bed after a big lunch and an afternoon of lovemaking. I don't know how long she had been standing there but I nudged Daniel and she walked to his side of the bed. They talked softly and intimately. I rose quietly and walked into the adjacent living area and dressed. Shortly after, Daniel followed and then we left. The woman's name was Eliane and she had been, up until then, Daniel's French girlfriend.

Bluebell arranged for us to see the show at the Lido, a surprisingly small room at the bottom of a red-carpeted stairway. Along with her sister cabaret, le Moulin Rouge, which boasts a much more colourful and lengthy history, the Lido is renowned for its dazzling review. The show was impressive for sure: a spectacular display of gaudy colour, leggy showgirls, ostrich feathers, diamantes and enormous stage sets. The dancers were truly captivating, the soloists, higher ranking dancers and the nudes adorned with sparkling jewellery cascading over their beautiful bodies as they glided across the stage.

In between rehearsals we had costume fittings and all the hullabaloo that goes with preparation for the opening of a show. Madame Bluebell was present for some of the rehearsals, overseeing the unfolding of the whole production with a meticulous eye. She was an elderly woman already but she didn't miss a beat and had no qualms about getting stern with any laziness. It was a busy time but I always loved the challenge and the satisfaction of rehearsals. At night I lay with Daniel in the dark, our bodies sticky from frenzied lovemaking and the summer heat. With him, at last, I felt meaningful exchange. We had a special connection, one that I had yearned for but so far had eluded me. We had grown close but it wasn't until the show was ready to leave for Portugal that I realised how much I was going to miss him.

'Don't worry, baby, my angel, I'll be here waiting for you, and I will call you,' he said. I didn't expect such seismic feelings and I certainly never anticipated being swept off my feet. But there it was—that euphoric, first flush of love—and it had begun on my very first day in Paris.

10

It was summer in Europe. The shores of the Mediterranean, all the way down the east coast of Spain to Marbella and across to Portugal on the west coast, were ablaze with the energy of revved-up holiday makers. At that time of year southern Europe transformed into a playground for the rich, the famous and the masses. The sun was shining; winter was gone and people descended on the coast to frolic and carouse in the holiday ambience.

Estoril Casino in Portugal was a 5-star resort nestled in a vast area of blossoming summer gardens. It boasted a reputation for being the largest casino in Europe, was the inspiration for Ian Fleming's *Casino Royale* and had an intriguing history as a gathering spot for espionage agents and dispossessed royals during World War Two. Juan Carlos, the entertainment manager, a tanned, silver-haired ladies' man, greeted us upon arrival. I took an instant dislike to his dismissive manner. He came across as arrogant and insensitive; he reminded me of my father. He was demanding and curt as he showed us restaurants, gift shops, the disco, cabaret rooms, and the pool, sauna and gym. We could take our meals in any of the restaurants within the casino or we could eat at a designated local restaurant as guests of the casino. As a lead, I was allocated my own double room with ensuite, pleasing enough I thought until I discovered there were no windows—with the casino completely booked out for the season we were all allocated rooms without windows. Apparently that didn't bother the others but I absolutely hated it. I felt claustrophobic immediately and worried about confinement in a room where I couldn't tell what time of day it was. Ruud found this most amusing and played a few practical jokes on me. He'd call me up pretending it was morning—'Come down to the pool. It's a beautiful sunny day'—when really it was the dead of night and vice versa. He nearly had me fooled a couple of times and while I appreciated his sense of humour I was not a happy camper.

We weren't a huge show: two leads, two boys and eight girls. We had two shows a night, the first in the main cabaret room and restaurant upstairs, and downstairs for the late show in a cosy cabaret room. Both stages were small in area so our rehearsal time was all about placement and realignment. The other lead dancer had starred at the Lido in Paris for some years and was far more experienced than me. She was also very beautiful, with an ice princess appeal, blue eyes and platinum-blonde hair, and she kept her distance, which I found unnerving.

Bluebell must have felt that I was up for the role otherwise she wouldn't have placed me alongside her but I couldn't find my feet and became agitated fairly early in the season. We had an impossible costume change that I thought I had grasped during rehearsal but couldn't quite manage on the night. I'd have everything laid out in the wings ready for the frantic race to disrobe and dress but no matter how organised I was, I never quite made it and appeared on stage a second or two late, supporting my ginormous, orange-feathered, mushroom-shaped headdress with one hand because I hadn't the time to pin it on properly. I was robbed of the chance to dance my best and that made me look silly. Juan Carlos noticed my tardiness and queried me about it in a derogatory tone, which made me feel even more stupid. I didn't often suffer a crisis of confidence when it came to dance but I began to experience feelings of inferiority.

The other lead must have seen I was having trouble with the changes and she must have sensed my anxiety, but she said nothing. I automatically assumed her indifference meant she had little regard for me. I practically handed her the psychological advantage, which in turn further diminished my sense of self-worth. It never occurred to me that she was threatened by me, that it was I who put her off. She may have been completely unaware of my trouble with the costume change but self-doubt niggled away in my mind nevertheless and instead of enjoying the show each night, I began to dread it. My usual confident, smiling performance was sabotaged by feelings of inadequacy. Cabin fever set in because of my windowless room. I felt trapped and disorientated. I suffered heart palpitations, a rising sense of panic and beads of sweat formed on my forehead. Melancholia was followed by bouts of absolutely terrifying fear.

Outside of work I sometimes went to the beach with Yolanda, one of the English dancers. There, we met a couple of surfer guys: Eduardo, a serious, intense man with a full head of jet black, shiny hair and deep acne scars around his chin, and his light-hearted mate, Rodriguez. They shared a house in town and although they spoke limited English they had been shaped by the same 70s beach culture values as me. They wore boardies and sandals; they burned incense and played music I'd grown up with. On bright, sunny mornings they drove us to beautiful, unpopulated surfing beaches up and down the coast and dropped us back at the casino in time for work; although there was one occasion when Yolanda and I both completely forgot about the afternoon matinee. We arrived in plenty of time for hair and makeup for the evening show but the moment we entered the dressing room, I wondered why all the other dancers' gear lay strewn about and the makeup lights were on. It looked as if everyone had already been there. Something was up. It took way too long for the penny to drop but slowly it dawned on me that while we had been swimming and sunbathing all day, oblivious to all else, we had missed the afternoon matinee. I gasped with shock. How could I have been so stupid? I had never just forgotten about work before and what astounded me most was that not at any time during the day did I have the slightest hint I was supposed to be at work. What a shocker that was. No one was impressed, although Ruud thought it was an absolute crack up.

On the surface Estoril shone as an ideal holiday destination but, behind the façade of tranquillity, civil strife was brewing. Portugal was emerging from a long dictatorship, and political rivalry had led to bombings and general social unrest. A threatening presence of armed militia randomly stopped and searched cars. They interrogated anyone they viewed as suspect. Eduardo and Rodriguez were targeted at a popular nightspot where Yolanda and I, being tall, blonde dancers and obviously foreign, were the focus of everyone's attention. Heavy-looking army guys carrying weapons stalked the place. And earlier, when we had pulled up in the car park, we were approached by armed police who, after brief questioning, searched the car. They were looking for weapons and explosives. The undercurrent of fear made me nervous and, for the first time ever, I began to understand how simple and safe life was in Australia. I remembered TV images of rallies against the Vietnam War and women protesting, demanding social equality, but it never occurred to me until then that democracy and civil peace is not a given.

Ruud and I spent a lot of time together. His good company and friendship helped ease my mind and quash my restlessness and intermittent feelings of panic. We took long walks around the city, cooled off in the pristine waters at sandy inlet beaches or watched local fishermen haul in the morning's catch. Things weren't right with me though. I started to linger in my hotel room and I called in sick for a few shows even though there was little evidence of anything physically wrong with me. The dance captain talked to me compassionately and thought perhaps I was homesick. I didn't know what was going on with me except that I was out of sorts and I didn't want to be in Estoril anymore.

Then Daniel called me. Ruud and I were lazing by the pool, sunning ourselves. It was early in the day and blindingly hot. Except for the two of us and the barman going about his duties in the poolside restaurant, the place was deserted and hushed until the shrill ring of the bar phone startled us out of our reverie. The barman called me over and I leapt up with excitement. I knew it must be Daniel; who else would be calling me poolside at the casino in Estoril? Who else would even know I was in Portugal?

"Ullo, baby, *mi amor*. How are you, my love? I miss you, my angel.'

I smiled at the sound of his voice; it was so good to hear him.

I told him everything about Portugal, the show, my windowless room and my unhappiness. I told him I didn't want to be there anymore, that I missed him too.

'Come back to Paris, Robs! I'll send you a ticket, baby; just tell me when you are ready.'

I wasn't even halfway into my contract. I couldn't possibly leave now.

'What am I going to do, Ruud? Maybe I can just bolt, you know, sneak out in the dead of night, do a bunk?'

'Don't be ridiculous,' he scoffed. He shook his head at the sheer lunacy of it. 'You can't. How will you get to Paris?'

'Hitchhike.'

'Hitchhike? Are you absolutely mad?' He laughed. 'You'll be murdered, or raped. Anyway, what will I do for the rest of the season without you?'

But Daniel had offered me a way out. Now that he had expressed his feelings and his desire for me to be with him, in my head I was already gone. Over the next couple of days I talked it over with Ruud. We spoke out of earshot from the others, as I tried to convince myself it was an acceptable option, while Ruud tried to talk me out of it. When Ruud eventually realised I had made my mind up to do a bunk, we got down to the nuts and bolts and hatched a plan. The only other person privy was Yolanda, who would accompany me out of the casino on my last night in Estoril. After the Sunday matinee, which would allow forty-eight hours to pass before anyone noticed my absence, Eduardo and Rodriguez would pick us up outside the casino and I would set out for Paris from their place early the following morning.

I decided to leave the bulk of my belongings behind with Ruud. I didn't need cumbersome luggage on the highway and I could always retrieve it later when we met up somewhere else in Europe. We consulted a map and I worked out that I would have to cut all the way through the guts of Spain to Madrid, head north to Biarritz and then inland and up the highway to Paris. I figured it would take three days, max.

When the time came for me to actually leave, I hesitated. The reality of the enormous plunge I was about to take hit me. Butterflies menaced my stomach, adrenalin pumped, but my optimism—or perhaps it was blind faith—and belief that good fortune would shine on me spurred me on. Ruud and I hugged tightly, holding on for as long as we could. I took a deep breath, gave a nod to Yolanda and off we scurried, swiftly ducking branches along the narrow pathway to the back entrance of the casino. I had this surreal sense that I was actually taking flight and as I did so my body relaxed and my mind changed gears. Suddenly I could see the funny side of this unfolding drama and I couldn't help but laugh at the absurdity of it all. What sort of a ratbag was I, stealthily fleeing in an outrageous move that would piss everyone off and seriously burn some bridges? We hurried through air thick with the scented perfume of summer gardens and stray insects buzzing. I looked anxiously for Eduardo's car and there he was, engine running, right on time.

Before I hit the road, Eduardo tried to get me to rethink my plan. Yolanda and Rodriguez slept soundly in the next room while we had a fitful night's sleep, tossing and turning. I couldn't get my mind off the journey ahead and Eduardo was annoyed because I refused to have sex with him. When he realised I was actually going to do this thing he spoke to me angrily.

'It's dangerous, Robyn. You just can't do this. It is not safe for a young blonde to be travelling alone on the highway, especially not in a short pair of cut-off jeans,' he said.

But it was no use. I'd made my mind up; I just wanted to get going now.

At first light I was up and running. Eduardo drove me to a good launching spot, wished me luck and embraced me firmly. As we parted, his normally severe face softened just a little and his eyes smiled at me warmly.

Hitchhiking to Paris all the way from Portugal—alone—was probably the stand out most stupid thing I ever did during my travels. I had some romantic, idealistic notion of experiencing a hitchhiking adventure similar to the ones I had read about in novels in my teens. I didn't grasp how dangerous it was and it never occurred to me that I had choices. I made my mind up and jumped into it with an urgency, as if life itself depended on it. I could have waited for Daniel to send me an air ticket or I could have finished off my contract then returned to a job at the Lido in Paris. Instead I didn't think at all. I reacted impulsively and impatiently. Deep down I was worried and uncertain about whether I could handle the season before me. Adopting a tough exterior and throwing myself into extreme action was my way of defying my fear. Growing up in our household, I learned reactionary behaviour rather than making informed, rational choices. Now in my ignorance and fear I was about to repeat that pattern.

11

*W*ithin minutes I managed to get my first ride, in a big semi-trailer. The brakes screeched loudly as the door flung open for me. I clambered up to the front carriage and slid in between the driver and his copilot. Just as we were about to exit the city onto the main artery out of Estoril, we came across a shocking road accident. Two cars were smashed up and a big truck lay on its side. One of its wheels still spun and there was an overpowering smell of petrol. Ambulances and tow trucks arrived, lights flashed and police sirens sounded. Blood-streaked victims groaned and curious passersby looked on in horror. It was a grim scene and I had to press fleeting thoughts of bad omens to the back of my mind.

We drove on away from the coastal breeze into the searing dry heat, past fields and scrub and small roadside villages across the border into the heart of Spain. The truck bounced and swayed. The noisy grind and splutter of the engine drowned out any conversation. I settled back and dozed off intermittently as we tore through mostly dry, barren countryside.

Late afternoon, we cruised into a sleepy little town and the end of my ride. The truck slowed to an amble. A burnt orange sunset cast long creepy shadows across stained white buildings that flanked the dusty streets. Ahead, three adolescent boys kicked a soccer ball around, red dust flaring up in its wake. Scanning the whole scene I wondered where all the people were. Except for the boys on the street, there didn't seem to be anyone around, just a ghostly silence. I had to decide whether to stay here overnight, or keep moving, which meant travelling into the darkness. Not such a good idea, I thought, but there was an air of desolation about this place and I didn't like the feel of it. As we rumbled down the empty street the teenage boys spotted me in the truck and came to an abrupt halt, oblivious to the ball rolling away into a ditch. They stared at me; penetrating glares that sent a shiver up my spine. The truck slowly negotiated a right-hand turn and, as we drove past, the boys locked eyes with mine. They did not take their eyes off me and I decided definitely to press on. These boys had seen me come into town and now I wanted them to see me leave.

I said goodbye to the two truckies on the outskirts of town, feeling vulnerable in my scant apparel. A cool dusk replaced the last of the sun's rays. I waited, scouring the surrounds while keeping my eye on the adolescent boys. A noisy truck with a canvas canopy chugged its way towards me. I hoped to God that this next lift was going to be a safe one.

As soon as I saw the driver my heart sank. He was a balding, middle-aged man with a sweaty face, big round bifocals and decaying teeth. He didn't look dangerous and he didn't feel dangerous with that silly little grin, but I wasn't sure. I glanced back at the teenage boys. Even from this distance I felt their intense stares follow my every move so, while the engine idled noisily, I looked back up again at this funny little man and decided to climb aboard. I placed my big red canvas carry bag at my feet and as I made myself comfortable I noticed his cargo: boxes and boxes of sweet-smelling peaches. I smiled and took that as a good sign; I'd made the right choice. This was a simple man, I told myself; too simple to be dangerous, I hoped. With one last glance at the adolescents and the ghostly town behind, the engine revved and we headed off into the guts of Spain.

The truck clattered and jigged along, bypassing small villages recognisable only by their lights in the distance. Even though I was in the middle of nowhere with a complete stranger who didn't speak English, I didn't feel scared or threatened. The night sky, sparkling with masses of stars, felt friendly and comforting. I did keep myself awake though, fighting off slumber in order to keep vigil, just in case. Eventually we came across a bustling truck stop with fluorescent lighting and garish neon signs and the funny little man pulled off the road and beside the bowsers. He filled up with petrol and then parked alongside rows of other trucks. Then the driver gestured for me to collect my things and to come inside with him to eat. I refused politely, preferring to wait it out in the truck, but he persisted. Ambling up to the restaurant, which was like a hamburger joint or roadside café, I could hear the grumble of conversation and the clatter of plates and cutlery inside, but the moment we entered all movement ceased and conversation hushed. The café was full of men eating dinner or drinking at the bar, probably all wondering what I was doing in a place like this looking like I'd just walked off the beach. Every eye in the place was on me. Necks craned to check me out as I walked to our table. Suddenly I was scared. I couldn't see any women, and there were no friendly faces. The funny little man ordered steaks, which we ate in silence while I wondered how I was going to handle the situation.

When we finished our meal the funny little man led me upstairs. I could feel the stares and curious gazes following us as we went. He led me along the corridor to a room, opened the door and indicated for me to go in. I froze momentarily, a look of pleading in my eyes, waiting, hoping for him to leave me, to retire to his own room. Suddenly he gestured that his room was down the hallway and left me. Phew! I thanked him and hurriedly locked the door behind me. It smelled stale and musty. The bed creaked and sank in the middle and was covered with a faded yellow chenille bedspread. A big timber wardrobe stood next to a bureau and chair and the bathroom reeked of phenol and rusty water pipes. Just as I was allowing myself to finally relax, a knock on my door stiffened me to attention. I didn't open it but recognised his voice immediately. It was him, the funny little man. I couldn't make out what he was saying but when I refused to open the door he knocked again, harder and louder this time and he was saying something to me in Spanish with a threatening tone. I opened the door just enough to be able to talk to him face to face but he pushed past me and placed himself on the bed.

'No . . . no,' I said. 'I'm going to sleep.'

He kept insisting, pointing to the bed. It was obvious what he wanted but there was no way I was going to let that happen. In our attempt to communicate, our gestures and arm movements began to resemble a game of charades but he was not budging at all and my initial fear morphed into anger. Did this ridiculous little toothless man seriously think I was going to have sex with him? He may have assumed me to be a pushover but that was a monumental misjudgement. Our arguing went on for some time, but my resolve and determination were steadfast. He finally realised I was not going to give in.

In the end, I won out and he stormed from my room, hissing and cussing as he went. Eventually everything went quiet. I waited with bated breath for a few moments then I heard him slam his door and descend the stairs, still cursing as he went. I dashed over to the window and saw his dilapidated truck chug off.

Everyone downstairs had heard this scenario unfold and now they must also know that I was alone. I was about 100 kilometres outside of Madrid, on a lonely highway at a remote truck stop full of strange men in the middle of the night. Realising my dilemma, a terrifying fear swallowed me up.

Frantically, I checked the lock on my door and pushed the furniture up against it. If someone tried to enter the room at least I would hear them first. As I lay under the covers I prayed like I had never prayed before. I'm not religious but there are times I wished I was and this was one of them. I begged God to look after me, pleaded with him to see me through the night safely. I thought of my mum and how angry she'd be with me for getting myself into this situation. What was I doing so far from home, drifting along a lonely highway all on my own? Tears welled up and suddenly I felt like a child, desperately needing the comforting embrace of a loved one.

I don't remember dozing off but I'll never forget waking up the next morning. I opened my eyes to sunshine beaming through the window. I looked over to the furniture, ridiculously out of place, still standing sentinel against the door. I was so happy to be alive and so relieved to be unharmed. I jumped up on the bed and threw the curtain open to see out the window. To my absolute astonishment and joy there were fields and fields of sunflowers as far as I could see. Masses of golden, smiling sunflowers danced, buffeted by a morning breeze. It was such a vision of beauty it felt like a gift from the heavens itself. I couldn't help believing at that moment that somewhere, someone or something was watching over me.

∽

With my confidence restored, I felt safe back on the road. Heading north, thick clusters of flowering bushes flanked the highway and what looked like poplars soared, giving way to sweeping farm landscapes. My driver, Etienne, was returning to Biarritz after visiting friends in a little town south of Madrid. His Renault was jam-packed with his belongings so it was a tight fit in the passenger seat. He had a thick, bushy beard and long hair messily tied into a ponytail, and he was the only Frenchman I had met who surfed. He reminded me of one of the surfie guys from my neck of the woods back on the Northern Beaches, except he seemed very serious and preoccupied. His face was strained and he whined rather than spoke, which made sense when he explained his girlfriend had just booted him out. After a while he lit a joint and we spoke of friends and of our lives, and I relaxed back to the wail of Bob Dylan on the cassette player.

We didn't arrive at Biarritz until well into the night so it was decided we'd sleep on the beach. One of us had to sleep outside on the sand and the other could lie stretched out on top of all the paraphernalia in the car. We took turns because neither spot offered comfort. Etienne graciously offered me the safety of the car first but halfway through the night we swapped, which was a welcome relief because it was too cramped and with only a few

98

centimetres between my face and the roof of the car I couldn't move. Snuggling up under a blanket on the sand I called out to Etienne in the car a few times just to reassure myself he was still there. I could tell by an emerging warm light and distant bird call that dawn wasn't far off, so I made myself comfortable and wondered what we would have done if it had been raining and cold.

Biarritz is more a bay than a beach but with small, nicely shaped little waves it is the closest thing you get to a surfing beach in France. The morning sun held the promise of a brilliant day ahead. Etienne and I sat silently on the beachfront checking the waves and demolishing a breakfast of warm croissants and thick, creamy coffee. While I looked out to the Atlantic on the south western tip of France, taking stock of where I was, geographically speaking, Etienne waxed up his board. We embraced, performed the ritual three cheek kisses and I hit the road again.

If I was lucky, I'd make it to Paris by late afternoon. I was more than halfway now, over the Spanish border and heading north. There hadn't been much passing traffic and, surrounded by a barren, dusty and deserted landscape, it felt eerily like I was traversing a moonscape. Save for the scorching sun and the flicker and buzz of stray insects for company, it was just me and the elements. Then I saw a figure come into view in the distance. I squinted and saw a darkly tanned man with dreadlocks and backpack trudging along in the other direction. We caught each other's eye and waved then the sound of a car engine and a speck of white moving towards me grabbed my attention. As it came closer I could see clearly a little white Fiat. It zoomed past, abruptly screeched to a halt about 25 metres ahead of me then noisily reversed to me on the side of the road. Four young men hung their smiling faces out the window.

'*Prego, bella, bella. Che bella.*' Italian, I deciphered. They jumped out to open the car door for me with such vigour I couldn't help but laugh. They were vibrant, charming and chivalrous and I noticed they were dressed stylishly in cool cotton shirts, jeans and expensive watches.

'Come on, get in.' They struggled with their limited English. 'You are safe with us.' Then they all burst out laughing, like what a joke that was. But then they did try to seriously reassure me that I would be delivered safe and sound as far as they could take me. I climbed in and, as we sped along with the windows down, a hot summer wind jetted at our faces, whipping our hair to and fro. In my best schoolgirl French—my French was better than their English—I conveyed my story to them and discovered they were university students returning to Rome after semester break. They were fun, animated and full of mirth and I relaxed, buoyed by their high spirits and enthusiasm. As promised, they delivered me safe and sound as far as they could take me and after much embracing and cheek kissing, we parted ways.

I watched the little Fiat disappear as the sun bore down, its searing heat burning my skin. I was dusty and dehydrated. My parched mouth stung and even though I was on the last leg of my journey I was tiring of it. The novelty had worn off and all I wanted was a shower and Daniel's warm embrace. Soon enough, another little car pulled up and a burly older woman with a long, greying plait and lots of facial hair stretched her arm through to the back seat and opened the door for me.

'Paris?' she asked.

'Yes, yes, thank you,' I replied, relieved to have come across a matriarchal type. Her husband, I presumed, was in the driver's seat and as I climbed in she nodded her head repeatedly and made hand movements like she was patting a dog.

'Sit, sit, sit,' she ordered. She handed me a flask of water and a pillow to rest my head and fussed over me like a mother. I laid back and rested my eyes, comfortable with the knowledge I was safe. Five hours later they dropped me off at Porte D'Italie.

Paris, at last! I'd arrived, dusty, dirty, tired but alive. I made my way across the road to a tabac and a public phone.

Fifteen minutes later my cab pulled up in Saint-Michel and there he was, my dark prince: tall and handsome with a wicked grin, just as I remembered him.

12

'*H*i, baby.' He swaggered up, elegantly dressed in a loose shirt, Levis, Ray-Bans with his Rolex glistening in the sun. He smiled, locking an arm into the small of my back and drawing me close to him. He leant over and kissed me with warm, tender lips then abruptly released his grip to pull out a roll of notes. He paid the driver, picked up my bag and took my hand. 'Come, my angel, let's go home to the "palace".'

Once out of the cab, I could feel his disapproving glare from behind his sunglasses.

'What do you think you are doing, hitchhiking all the way from Portugal and why didn't you wait for me to send you airfare?'

I looked at him blankly and blushed like a child does when they are unable to adequately explain.

'Goddamn, that is a crazy thing you did, Robyn,' he scolded, shaking his head as we ambled past busy cafés and carefree people out and about, enjoying the summer weather.

I lowered my eyes, feeling slightly silly, and said nothing.

'And you can't get around like that, Robyn; we are in Paris. People here dress elegantly. You look like fresh meat on display.'

Then he watched the faces of people who were all checking us out as we walked past. 'You see? Everyone is looking at you,' he said angrily. 'I'm going to have to take you shopping, Robs.'

Daniel had relocated since our last meeting. Up in his third-floor apartment, one street back from the heart of Saint-Michel, he led me into a living room flooded with sunlight by floor-to-ceiling windows. It had a full bathroom, a roomy kitchen and an ornate fireplace where Daniel had stashed thirty thousand American dollars. He made a point of letting me know that in case I had to access it for any reason. (From the two balconies I could see into the apartments directly opposite and catch glimpses of the Seine, alive with barges and tour boats, Île de la Cité and the spires of majestic Notre-Dame down the road. A hot shower washed away the grime and crud from three days on the road and then I seated myself on the balcony to dry off my hair in the sun while Daniel watched me from the low bed. He gestured.

'Come here, my baby. Come lie me with me.'

I moved closer and knelt at the side of the bed. He took my hand and pulled me to him to kiss my forehead and my eyes, and to sweep my hair off my shoulders. We touched and smiled with a tenderness and affection that lit up my heart. We crashed into each other's arms, spellbound by that rush of love. It was more than sex, it was a compelling intimacy; a sense of belonging, of comfort. The touch of his skin, his gentle, masculine hands, his groans of pleasure. My hair tumbling down over my breasts as I slid over him and then he took command, throwing me over, bearing down and I surrendered to him.

Anne, a Danish girl and an acquaintance of Daniel's, lived across the square in a modest little apartment overlooking a small plaza of cafés, bars and restaurants. She lived with Guy, an American man I didn't immediately take to, but I trusted Anne as soon as I met her; her cropped red hair, smiley personality and petite frame reminded me of an elf. She was gracious and charming and in no time at all we became good friends. The four of us started to hang out and frequently gathered for dinner or to take in a film at the Saint-Germain cinema. From their balcony we drank champagne and watched the fireworks and colourful celebrations for Bastille Day. When Anne told me she had scored tickets to see the Paris Opera Ballet performing *Swan Lake* open air at the Louvre, Daniel saw the excitement in my face and decided we must join them. This was Rudolf Nureyev's ballet company dancing to Tchaikovsky's score—for me, it was a spellbinding event. I'd seen *Swan Lake* a couple of times but there in Paris, with the dramatic backdrop of the Louvre, the unfolding love story of passion and trickery and the moving pas de deux, tears welled in my eyes. There I sat, arm in arm with Daniel, totally swept up in the romance and beauty of the ballet, and entranced by the newness of our promising love.

We spent most mornings making love. Daniel was enraptured with my tight dancer's body and bewitched with my 'innate sexiness', as he called it. He liked me getting about scantily clad or frolicking on our big bed so he could photograph my 'naked beauty'. We couldn't get enough of each other. His adoration was addictive, not that I recognised it as that. I slid into a comfort zone with him and allowed myself to drown contentedly in his affection.

We read *The Washington Post* and *Newsweek*. He opened my mind to politics, the super powers, South American culture, Fidel Castro and Che Guevara. Apart from Santana and the Latin-flavoured music of South America and Cuba, his music tastes were straight compared to mine: his adolescence was shaped by the sounds of Frank Sinatra, Elvis Presley and Roy Orbison. Just for me, he managed to score tickets to see David Bowie, the Rolling Stones, Fleetwood Mac and John McLaughlin. At home back in the palace he would entertain me, in his boxers, with his rendition of 'Oh, Pretty Woman'. He was fun and playful and I loved him for it.

We did go shopping as promised. Apparently Daniel knew models and other beautiful women who gave him inside tips on where we should shop. He wanted me to look as good as anyone else in Paris and soon my casual attire was replaced with chic, elegant apparel. Not everyone in Paris wears haute couture but the Parisians know how to dress. I learned that classic style transcends time, that less is more, simple is elegant, and a great jacket is essential.

Further into the summer season we took off to the south of France to Peillon, a fortified village perched high atop a rocky peak in the hinterland of La Côte d'Azur. Vaulted passageways, a bell tower and a labyrinth of cobblestone pathways and narrow stairs led to private bungalows and a restaurant with sweeping views of the countryside. Daniel's friend Pierre, who Daniel referred to as *Pedro*, and his girlfriend, Francoise, a petite blonde who didn't speak English, joined us. Each morning we drove down the mountain to spend the day on the beach or to stroll along the boulevards. Huge hotel complexes leased out the beachfronts and for a fee (shock, horror!) you could enter and hire a sunbed. The beaches had grey pebbles instead of sand, and their warm waters, after clean, crashing Pacific Ocean waves, were an unremarkable experience. The most obvious differences to the beach scene at home were the lack of surf and how dressed up everyone was: designer swimwear, jewellery, bling-bling sunnies. Topless women, tanned, potbellied old men and young playboy types packed the shores of the Mediterranean. Flashy speed boats and sleek yachts adorned with scantily clad women cruised by. Everyone was so busy checking everyone else out; it felt like we were part of a major fashion event, or a circus, or a movie set.

At the end of sun-drenched days lolling about among the chic set, we wound our way back up the mountain to our bungalows, dressed for dinner and dined al fresco on the balcony restaurant. We could see the lights of Nice shimmering in the distance and it was here, in this most enchanting of settings, that Daniel announced his intentions to marry me. My heart surged and I became dreamily spellbound by the romance of it but then he added: 'Robs, if anything goes wrong at least we have had our honeymoon.'

I didn't understand what he meant, and though there was a hint of doom laced in there, I felt it would be too silly to query him about it.

By the time we arrived back in Paris, Jenny had returned from Hong Kong and she and Diego became part of our social circle. In fine restaurants with white linen tablecloths or at the rustic tables of a brasserie we dined on pâté de foie gras, crudites, or hearty *lapin* dishes. Daniel liked steak tartare; I could never come at that. I preferred coq au vin, Chateaubriand and escargot drowning in garlic and butter. We dined quite late each night and usually did cocaine afterwards then headed off to a club, where we mixed it up with the uber cool set of Paris until the early hours of the morning. In fashionable Saint-Germain-des-Pres we drank coffee at Les Deux Magots, and sipped Kir Royal or absinthe at Café de Flore. We ate club sandwiches at Le Drugstore, which housed a pharmacy, restaurant and supermarket all under the same roof.

There were no responsibilities; no pattern of work, eat, sleep. Day flowed into night and night into morning. No one worked but there was always money for anything we needed. I was a world away from my simple beach life back home. In Australia, Italian cuisine was only just beginning to subtly alter our diet of meat and three veg. Chiko rolls, hamburgers, fish 'n' chips and milkshakes were the lunchtime fare at our beachside takeaway joints.

My attachment to Daniel grew swiftly. He made me laugh and I loved his warm, gregarious nature. I was beguiled by my new sophisticated lifestyle and his lavish attention, although he fretted that my unpretentious manner made me vulnerable. He was certain that my naivety, pretty young face and slender figure made me an easy target for seedy characters and were therefore good reasons for him to protect me against the brittle reality of life. Up until then it never occurred to me that my natural allure was anything to fear or be ashamed about, but his messages began to change the way I felt about myself. He berated me for my innocence and drilled me intensely about the manner in which I should present myself. I liked that in those early days; I thought it showed he cared about me. No man had ever deliberately set out to protect me so ardently before.

During those first months spent together the dynamics of our relationship were established. I was emotionally vulnerable to him and had already, albeit subtly, allowed him to undermine my sense of self-worth. He manoeuvred me deftly into a subordinate role with his whole macho dominant male act. I allowed him to ply me; I was malleable and thought I could handle it; after all, I was familiar with the experience of dominating men. I did not recognise it but my life had begun to slide into decline.

13

*O*ne warm, sunny afternoon at Jenny's place, I lay on the couch sunning myself in brilliant rays of early autumnal light. I was daydreaming, thinking about Peillon and Daniel's declaration that he would marry me, when Jenny called out, jolting me out of my reverie.

'Robyn, I've got to go out. I have a few errands to run. I won't be long.'

I heard the door slam behind her and then the lift door clang shut in the hallway outside. I got up lazily and walked out onto the little balcony to watch her leave, squinting in the bright sun. Clusters of pigeons cooed away while sunning themselves on surrounding rooftops. I stayed there for a few moments, then walked outside and slumped over the iron railing with my arms dangling, and glanced down to see Jenny approach her little orange BMW. As she inserted the key, three men dressed in suits appeared and surrounded her. That seemed odd.

I stood up immediately, more alert now, and the phone rang. I dashed back inside to answer it, found no one on the other end and rushed back to the balcony to discover Jenny and the three men had disappeared. Confusion had barely set in when the apartment door burst open and the three men stormed in with Jenny firmly in their grasp. I stood watching, stupefied, while they tore the place apart. My heart jumped into my throat as the apartment was ransacked. Every single nook and cranny was searched. Drawers were emptied, clothes tossed. Books ripped, mattresses knifed; all sorts of stuff went flying to the ground. Vigorous interrogation of each of us in separate rooms followed.

It was a bust—these guys were narcotics agents and that phone call had been a ploy to distract me before I had a chance to flee. Not that I would have; I had nothing to hide. I cooperated willingly, complying with their demands and playing dumb, as if I didn't know anything, which was the truth after all—I had no clue as to what they were after and no information to impart.

Jenny was handcuffed and taken into custody and I was left reeling. For the next several hours I paced around that apartment, smoking nervously, tidying up and waiting to hear from Daniel. I didn't know what I was supposed to do so I just waited; I knew he'd call and eventually he did.

"Ullo, Robs, my angel. Are you okay?'

Then he asked me to go to a public phone and call him, where he milked me for every detail about what had transpired. I told him all that I could recall.

'My love, my love, please listen to me! Okay, Robyn, say nothing about this to anyone. Do not talk to anyone on the home phone and, whatever you do, do not trust anyone. Do you hear me, Robyn? Don't even trust Jenny. They may be after Diego, Robs, and Jenny will betray me. They will threaten her and she will squeal on me to save her boyfriend. And *mi amor, por favor*, always call me on a public phone, make sure no one is hovering behind you, listening to your conversation, and check to see if you are being followed. Can you get out of Paris for a while just until this all blows over, my angel? It will be safer for you. I love you, Robs.'

Get out of Paris? Where did he think I could go to at such short notice? I had no work lined up, no family close by, apparently no safe place to stay, no money and no idea when I was going to see him again.

Later that night Jenny was released. She returned to the flat with some cash for me. Diego had retrieved it from the fireplace in Daniels' apartment along with my belongings. I didn't know any of the details surrounding the episode that day but I took Daniel at his word and clung onto them as if they were my lifeline. I loved him and knew he loved me back. I wasn't going to let go. Many years later, when I learned of the circumstances leading up to the raid that day, I wondered if I would have made different choices in the ensuing months had I known the true nature of what was going on. Daniel was expecting ten kilograms of cocaine to arrive at Charles De Gaulle Airport from Bogotá. A Colombian girl was carrying the contraband in two suitcases with false bottoms but the luggage had been mistakenly tagged to go to Puerta Rico. When no one arrived to retrieve the luggage in Puerta Rico, closer scrutiny by customs discovered the coke. Narcotic agents were notified, the bags were sent to Paris and the next day, when the Colombian girl retrieved the luggage she was arrested. Daniel was at the airport that day and witnessed the arrest taking place from a distance. The girl was interrogated and milked for information, which in turn led to the raid on Jenny's place that day. It was only a matter of time before the narcs found their way to Daniel. He was subsequently arrested for trafficking and, after many months in gaol, he hired a second lawyer who argued that the crime had been committed outside French territory so the charge was null and void. Daniel was a free man again. In the meantime I called my friends in the UK.

Christine and Paul lived in Surrey, south of London. They were the closest thing to family on this side of the planet and I knew I could call on them. I'd become good friends with Christine while working with her at South Juniors back in Sydney and Paul was a mate of my eldest brother's and a familiar face from the Peninsula. I'd introduced them and now they were married.

When I called them to explain my predicament I deliberately kept much of the sordid details to myself. I knew Christine wouldn't be impressed, but I had to cough up the basics and convey to her my sense of urgency.

'What on earth have you got yourself caught up in?' she demanded.

Then I pressed her for any leads she might have about work in the UK.

'Well, incredible as it sounds, Robyn, you're in luck.'

My heart leapt with anticipation.

'A very good friend of mine,' she continued, 'just happens to be looking for a dancer for *The Dick Emery Show*. She needs someone right away for the rest of the summer season and I am absolutely astounded at your impeccable timing. How soon can you get here?'

I used the time on the flight over the Channel to think about how I was going to adequately explain myself to friends I hadn't seen in several years. Predictably, Christine fired a tirade of questions and advice at me and Paul listened but stayed cool. He and I shared a cavalier 'she'll be right' Northern Beaches' attitude and were able to irreverently play down the gravity of my situation with humour. Besides we had more important things to discuss: I needed to know the details of this job.

The Dick Emery Show, Christine explained, needed an immediate replacement dancer for its summer season in Blackpool at the BBC Theatre. One of the dancers was having a nervous breakdown and wanted to leave the country. Coincidentally, she was an Australian girl and her name was Robyn. Because I didn't have an equity card it was illegal for me to work anywhere in the UK, but sharing the same name and nationality as this girl meant I could step into her role as she slipped out without the authorities knowing. I couldn't believe my good fortune, and timing.

Christine had already arranged for me to meet Roger, the agent, and I didn't have time to change or glam up after the flight. My Levi's, cerise kimono shirt and strappy pewter high heels would have to do. Paul, deciding to give me a tour of London en route to Roger's, bulleted the car into the congested London traffic. The car lurched from lane to lane, dodging red double-decker buses and black cabs. We whizzed past Buckingham Palace, Big Ben, Marble Arch and Hyde Park. London was alive with energy, bustling and crowded with a diverse mix of people.

Handsome and debonair, Roger rose from his chair, walked around his big solid desk and looked me up and down. Greetings and introductions ensued. He lowered himself on to the edge of his leather-topped desk, crossed one ankle over the other, folded his arms and lowered his head to peer at me over his specs. Then he zoomed in on my face and asked me about my experience. I relayed all the relevant guff and after a few moments he returned to his seat, sat down and leant back to dial Maz Jeacle, a smug look on his face. Maz was a highly regarded Australian artist who had been living and working in Europe for some time and, for this season, was the choreographer for *The Dick Emery Show*. Furthermore, she just happened to be the sister of Ken Jeacle, the choreographer I had worked with at Souths Juniors in Sydney.

'Well . . . she's tall, blonde and beautiful, Maz,' he said into the receiver, 'and she's been a Bluebell.'

Roger paused, looking up from the receiver and over to me. 'She wants to know if you can dance?'

'Dance? Can I dance?' I asked with mock indignation. 'I can dance, no worries about that, I can dance.'

He laughed. 'She says, yes, she can dance.'

They carried on their conversation for a few minutes while Chris, Paul and I talked among ourselves. I took note of the photos posted around the room, stars and celebrities Roger had managed, I presumed, then he hung up the phone and addressed me.

'Okay then, Robyn, you're in. We leave the day after tomorrow—you'll drive with me.'

With that finalised, Chris, Paul and I jumped back into the car, launched into catch-up prattle and hastened out of the city, onto a narrow country road that wound its way over quaint bridges and babbling brooks through lush green English countryside. We passed Tudor-style estates, an enchanting thatched-roof house and stately homes with flourishing gardens. The light drizzle from an overcast sky was exactly the sort of weather I'd anticipated. All that was missing were the bloodhounds and horses and riders in pursuit of an elusive fox.

To be able to climb into a comfy bed with a plan in place was sheer bliss. I lay there in the solitude of my room going over all the dizzying details of the past two days in my mind. One minute I had been sunning myself peacefully at Jenny's apartment in Paris, the next, there is a drug raid, narcotic agents, a ransacked flat, aggressive interrogation and scrutiny. Jenny is hauled off for questioning about Diego, but it is Daniel, my lover, who is incarcerated. I was so relieved to be with old friends and on my way to the BBC Theatre to do *The Dick Emery Show*.

14

*F*rom the moment we met I recognised Maz to be down to earth, honest and unpretentious. She welcomed me into her flat and showed me my room and we got to work straight away. I had five routines to learn and, with the emergence of sunshine, a rarity in the normally overcast skies of Blackpool, we decided to rehearse in the leafy courtyard. Maz was visibly relieved when I picked up her choreography quickly and easily; after all, I hadn't even auditioned for this job. Her choreography, theatre jazz, was easy to enjoy and a pleasure to dance and she was genuinely impressed with the quality of my performance. Once I had all the routines worked out, we rehearsed at the theatre so she could get a good look at me up on stage. I'll never forget her smile and encouraging words: 'Oh, Robyn, it is so refreshing to come across a dancer with style and strong technique.'

After all the drama I'd been through, her praise uplifted my spirits enormously. I learnt a new routine each day and by the end of the week I was fully immersed in the show and happy, not only because I had landed on my feet but also because in Maz I had met a genuine friend.

Blackpool is a funny little place, a seaside city and a popular holiday spot for working-class Brits; it reminded me of Tuggerah Lakes or Toukley on New South Wales' Central Coast. During the day, kids played while their dads fished on wide wooden piers running far out to sea. Gannets squawked and families gobbled up steaming fish 'n' chips from butcher's paper. Greyish black pebbly sand crunched underfoot as I made my way to the murky shore that I practically needed a pair of binoculars to spot, it was so far out. Apart from the pantomimes and theatre productions showing for the summer season, a big attraction in Blackpool are the Illuminations. All the way along the six-mile beachfront promenade a display of kitsch lamps and festoons lights up the city at night and draws crowds of local families and die-hard visitors. I thought they were garish but the locals love them.

Life soon fell into a simple routine. Maz and I shopped for groceries at the village square, we cooked humble meals and we washed the dishes each evening before work. During the day we did some scenes for the film production of the next Dick Emery television series at nearby locations. Maz and I got on well. We yacked about life, our loves and our dilemmas. She was going through her own reinvention at that time and had big choices to make. I started writing poetry; it brought a sense of relief and order to what was shaping up to be my rollercoaster ride of a life.

Each night before curtain when the lights dimmed and there was that moment's hush from the audience just before the orchestra starts, Dick Emery emerged from the darkness of the wings to wish the cast a very good evening. I was impressed by that and astonished at his gracious demeanour. I was well aware of his thirty-year reputation as a light entertainment icon but my recall of him was of the comic, grotesque characters he portrayed in the television series—to find him well spoken, charming and refined was an unexpected surprise.

It was during intermission before curtain that Dick first approached me.

'Good evening, young lady,' he said, taking my hand and kissing it. I smiled and chatted with him and I knew instantly that he was flirting with me.

This exchange steadily became a nightly ritual, one that I began to look forward to. He'd appear from the wings and saunter over with a twinkle in his eye, engaging me with his humour, and we'd chat. One evening, he asked me if I'd care to take a flight with him in his private plane for a bird's eye view of the surrounding countryside, which he assured me was truly breathtaking from the air. It did sound like fun but he was thirty-odd years older than me and I wondered about his intentions once we were sky high. I half-heartedly accepted his invitation because I lacked the confidence to graciously turn him down but at the eleventh hour I backed out. His frisky enthusiasm towards me soured to disappointment instantly.

After my refusal, our intermission ritual diminished to little more than perfunctory acknowledgement. I felt rotten about it but then he did something really touching. The last night of the show, he presented me with a gift. A rust-coloured corduroy lion, with a woolly mane, a mascot (one too big to pack away) to carry with me everywhere. He wanted this lion to always remind me of him. When I stooped to kiss him on the cheek, he was coy and sweet and wished me all the very best of luck.

That last night in Blackpool I danced my heart out. Christine and Paul had mutual friends of ours from Australia staying with them and they'd driven up from London to see the show. I was so excited to see friends from home and I really wanted to strut my stuff. But back at the flat I became a bit morbid. My mood altered after we smoked a joint and reminisced about home and the good old days on the Peninsula.

The end of a season always brought on a touch of the blues, a bit like the end of anything in life, but I was anxious about my precarious situation. I usually had somewhere to jump to and friends to jump with and it seemed everyone except me had plans. With winter ahead and a heart aching, longing to be with Daniel again, it was hard to stave off feelings of despair. I tossed and turned that night, wondering what I was going to do. Roger had offered me a cabaret job in Madrid that I initially had agreed to do but it sounded tacky and cheap so later I turned him down, which really pissed him off. I'd heard The Talk of the Town, a fashionable London cabaret, was auditioning and *A Chorus Line*, which was playing at Drury Lane theatre in London, was after a dancer for the 'tits and arse' character but I had no acting or singing experience. Even if I'd got the chance to wing it, I didn't have an equity card and that counted me out.

The drive back to London the next day was dismal. Maz had issues with her fiancé, which worried her into a heavy silence and all I had was a phone number of a woman in Amsterdam, Helen LeClercq, with whom I might find a job; a flimsy lifeline the girls in *The Dick Emery Show* had given me. As we drove on, deep in our own dark thoughts, storm clouds gathered, and heavy rain pelted down noisily. The windscreen wipers clocked furiously back and forth. It was miserable. Roger had offered Maz and I his flat in London for one night but now that I had reneged on the Madrid gig he rescinded his invitation to me. I don't know what I would have done that night if Maz hadn't insisted I ignore his cold shoulder and stay there with her anyway. Even so, with only one night's grace in London, the pressure was on for me to make up my mind about what I was going to do. The world seemed suddenly scary and slippery and by the time we reached Roger's flat I was on the verge of tears. When I finally drifted off to sleep, my mother's voice echoed in the recesses of my mind. As a kid, whenever I was emotionally overwrought, she always reassured me that after a good night's sleep the world would be brighter.

She was right. Next morning, I woke rested and in a more rational state of mind. A good night's sleep hadn't altered my tricky situation but I was feeling more optimistic and so made the call to Helen LeClercq in Amsterdam to arrange a meet. Maz was on the move early, on her way home to the Channel Islands and I too had to keep moving. We said our goodbyes at Waterloo Station and with my lion underarm I took the train south to Dover, then the ferry across the Channel to Calais and from there I picked up another train that took me all the way to Paris.

I met with Jenny and Diego briefly, hoping there was news of Daniel but there was nothing. All they told me at the time was that Daniel had been arrested, but was being held on false charges. They stressed that I had to be patient, that he would be a free man soon. Diego passed on Daniel's message of amorous sentiment, which was intended to sustain me until Daniel's release. Then he gave me more cash and the contact details of a friend in Amsterdam and I jumped a train for the five-hour trip.

I was nervous about what lay ahead for me in Amsterdam but as the train cut through vast fields of rich farmland I was comforted by the rhythmic clickety clack; it settled my angst. At least I had a job prospect to look forward to, I thought, and willed myself into a positive state of mind. At some point I had to contact my mother but I didn't want to divulge all the details of my precarious situation, so I decided to put that off until I was in work again.

15

$\mathcal{H}$elen LeClercq Dance Studio was located on one of the three main canals running through the heart of Amsterdam. The studios commanded the entire ground floor area, Helen resided in an expansive middle-floor apartment above, and a couple of African-American jazz musicians from New York who were doing gigs around town occupied the atelier studio. At our first meeting, I auditioned, and Helen offered me a job teaching contemporary dance without hesitation and accorded me the loft apartment, a small attic with a little window overlooking the roofs and spires of the city. I had to share the bathroom and kitchen with the musicians on the floor below—an acceptable compromise, I thought, considering my lack of funds and displaced status.

I taught evening classes for adult beginner to intermediate levels in jazz and contemporary dance, drawing on the Graham and Horton technique I'd studied at Bodenwieser's. I picked up enough of the language to communicate to the students in Dutch although I soon discovered that everyone in Amsterdam speaks English, French and German. In time, Helen offered me a spot with her professional group, the Helen Le Clercq Dancers. We did cabaret gigs in the Netherlands and Germany but the work was sporadic and the pay paltry.

My relief at having secured a job and a place to stay gave me reason to be mildly optimistic but my life in Amsterdam was miserable. I entered a lonely phase where I wandered aimlessly around the city like a lost soul; up cobblestone streets and over narrow arched bridges, past Anne Frank's hideaway, houseboats, galleries, shops and cafés, including one that dated as far back as the seventeenth century, and others where you could buy dope with your coffee. With the coming of dreary weather and chill winds, I too seemed to take on a grey hue. As the colder months set in I sank into melancholia and took up writing poetry again in the solitude of my little room or stayed warm in a café up the road with an American girl I met at class. We filled up on cheese, wholemeal fruit buns and thick coffee with koffiemelk.

I rang Diego's contact, Jack, who was expecting my call. He had dark curly hair, steely blue eyes and a house with a huge living area for perpetual partying. It had a pool table, a foosball table (the game with the levers and the plastic players), backgammon and a chess set. A TV remote hung from the ceiling on a piece of elastic and hovered over the centre of a round table always strewn with a mull bowl, papers, a mirror and razor blade, and ashtrays overflowing with cigarette butts: remnants of the previous night's carousing. A huge TV screen dominated the room and there were always heaps of people at Jack's place, and lots of cocaine, grass, hashish, and movies playing and music blaring. At our very first meeting Jack tried to seduce me on the couch, which stunned me, because moments later his model girlfriend, who had been asleep in the next room, came out to introduce herself. During the day the curtains were drawn to keep out the light but at night the house came alive. It was a wild house with wild people.

I was out of my depth with these hardcore party animals but I tagged along with Jack and his ever present entourage of friends to see Santana playing live in a club in the heart of the city and to see Peter Frampton in concert in a big stadium on Amsterdam's outskirts. I'd surrounded myself with all these people to feel a sense of belonging but I was hanging out with the wrong crowd and I felt even more lonely. I missed Daniel terribly and hung on for news of his release. Any day now, I kept telling myself, any day now he will send for me. The prospect of a happy reunion with him kept me going and even though all I had to cling on to was a dreamlike memory of romantic love, I was unyielding. My life had shrunk to the barest minimum and my vulnerability predisposed me to making the most diabolical decisions.

I was poking around in the musicians' flat downstairs one morning, snooping around really, when I came across some American money in the kitchen drawer. I was broke, cold and hungry and when I saw those notes I thought perhaps I could borrow them, just until Helen got back from an out-of-town business thing, just until our next gig. I had no intention of stealing and I hesitated for a brief moment, a warning voice tinkled away in my head, but I grabbed the money and headed to the train station to buy some guilders. I could replace them with my next pay I thought. It never occurred to me that the bills were counterfeit.

So there I was, standing in a queue of about ten people in the deafening station mayhem. I was a bit edgy; after all this was not my money and I hadn't asked anyone if I could borrow it. At the perspex barrier I handed over my dollars to a woman who looked at the money, then looked up at me and asked me to wait a moment. She disappeared out the back, which I thought was a bit curious.

Then suddenly I was pulled out of the queue, my hands were cuffed, two armed guards seized my elbows and pushed my head down and I was hauled off through a crowd of gawkers. I struggled to lift my head, to free my arms and to make sense of what was happening. I called out in protest and pleaded to know what I had done. I was shoved into a paddy wagon and taken off to the local police station. A urine-soaked cell was my home for the night. I was shocked and scared to find myself locked up in a dingy hole meant for real criminals.

The next morning the chief sat me down in his office and questioned me. I coughed up the truth and pleaded my innocence. The police chief thought perhaps someone had put me up to it. He confirmed my story with Helen, then let me go, directing one of his cops to escort me home in a police vehicle, although I wasn't out of the woods yet. I had some serious explaining to do to Helen, who took pity on me. She thought perhaps I had taken the money for drugs or for a friend needing it for drugs and I had to convince her of the prosaic nature of my behaviour.

Right about then life took an upward swing all on its own. The winter weather had begun to melt away and the hint of spring in the air brought with it my buddy Ruud Vermeij. To my great relief, Ruud had finished the gig at the casino in Estoril and was back in the Netherlands. His arrival and his friendship were a huge boost to my morale. He was living with his boyfriend in Breda and at his invitation I often took the train to their place to spend several days with them. It was like having a family member close by; his company fortified my ailing spirit. As for the bag of clothes I had left in his care in Estoril? It was gone, stolen by one of the other dancers. She'd had her eye on it from the moment I left, he said, and had snuck off with it when no one was watching. What a disappointment that was, all my beautiful tailor-made clothes from Hong Kong and my cheongsam gone forever!

Still, they were only clothes and my disappointment about that was short lived. Rehearsals for a huge production at Le Marre Theatre had wrapped up and the show was about to go live. This was a send-off performance for Helen, who was retiring and taking off with her partner to Africa. It showcased all of Helen's past and present dance works and featured all the students and professionals who had worked with her over the years, including musicians and dramatic art segments. There was a brilliant and memorable contemporary ballet to Pink Floyd's *Dark Side of the Moon*, some funky jazz routines and a classical repertoire. Once this performance was over I was going to be out of a job and a flat but luckily Ruud put me in touch with a Dutch guy, Jan Arntz, who was auditioning dancers for a job in Milan.

I was in the opening number and had already taken my place on stage at Le Marre when Helen beckoned me from side stage. I dashed over to find out what was up and there, standing in the wings, was my friend Bron, who I hadn't seen or heard from since Hong Kong. I could hardly believe it. She had seen my name on the program and made her way past the doorman and all the dressing rooms backstage to let me know she was in the audience. I was absolutely elated to see her. We couldn't contain our squeals of glee and agreed to rendezvous later that evening in the piano bar at the American Hotel next door.

The bar was charged with excitement that night, packed with all the performers, musos and stage crew from the show. Everyone was smoking furiously and engaged in highly animated conversation. Over the noise of excited jabber, I learnt Bron was in town doing a show at a little club up the road. She too was broke and from what she told me I don't think the show she was doing carried much prestige, so I talked her into auditioning with me for Jan Arntz. She agreed and on the day dragged along a couple of other dancers, Dutch girls who were keen to live and work in Italy. Jan's studio was a long trek out of Amsterdam by train and the audition was a little tricky because his choreography was quirky and I could tell straight away that he was a bit eccentric too.

He hired us all that day and I remember feeling a surge in optimism. For months I'd dragged my heart around in a heavy cloak of sadness. I'd felt as if I was being swallowed up by despair but now spring was on the way. I had a job lined up in Milan and in the company of my good friend Bron; my spirits soared.

16

*J*an Arntz's strong face featured dark, shapely
eyebrows and a big nose and he kept his shiny black hair
slicked back from a broad forehead. At rehearsals he wore a
tight Bonds-style singlet revealing his muscular, well-developed
dancer's torso, with high-waisted trousers and dance sneakers.
His physical resemblance to Freddie Mercury was striking. But
Jan was a ballroom dancer, something he began in his father's
studio as a child, which led to competitions and then eventually
to teaching. Now he wanted to do a big show. He had ideas for
a glamorous extravaganza, a production to show off the boy
dancers as much as the girls.

La Cupola D'oro, a huge dome-shaped building, was the newest
cabaret venue in Milan and for the show Jan had designed a
glossy, black, tiered stage set with lots of mirrors and sparkling

drapes reminiscent of a 30s speakeasy. There was much press about it; television crews came in to film our dress rehearsals, which were flashed across prime-time screens. (My little boobs in particular, apparently. I didn't see it but everyone told me about it afterwards.) And there were radio broadcasts and newspaper features promoting the new spectacular. We were a multinational cast, though mostly Dutch. There twenty dancers in all, including a South American; two English girls; Uta, a stern older German woman; Bozena, a pretty Polish girl; a South African; and three Aussies—Bron, Peter Pan and myself. Pete was tall, good looking, very masculine and one of the strongest and most appealing male dancers I'd ever come across. He also happened to be one of only two straight men I ever came across in all my experience as a dancer and I was pleased to be partnered with him for most of the production numbers. Jan's boyfriend, Eric—a tall, platinum blond American man and a very strong dancer—had a mythical look about him, a half-man, half-horse thing. Joan, an aging, long-standing friend of Jan's, was appointed dance captain.

We had brand-new glitzy costumes adorned with pearls, diamantes and rhinestones. Sparkling headdresses with colourful plumage lit up the stage. For the girls, Jan demanded dark, Twiggy-style eyes and shaved eyebrows, which were replaced with glitter. The boys had to paint on moustaches and slick their hair back. I was a lead and danced opposite Nikki, one of the other three leads, usually up front. She and I were often first out on stage to greet excited audiences with our fast-paced jazzy opening. We entertained them with a big production, a comedy piece from *Funny Girl* and three of the boys donned drag and amused audiences with their playful impersonation of the Andrew Sisters' 'Boogie Woogie Bugle Boy'. Serge, the French magician, baffled and mesmerised audiences with his incredible powers of illusion. Frenchy, the trapeze artist, performed death-defying feats, an awe-inspiring spectacle of balletic acrobatics high above in the cupola and Anne, the red-headed chanteuse and trapeze artist's lover, belted out her repertoire with the ten-piece band.

Jan was a passionate, creative man and at times quite eccentric. He had to have things just as he wanted them; he was intense and demanding. His stylised Bob Fosse–inspired choreography proved very tricky and every so often his temper flared when the frustration of not getting what he wanted out of his dancers became too much. His temperamental turns never bothered me because I always gave him what he wanted and, besides, I was used to aggressive, overbearing men losing their cool. But gosh he could be an absolute bastard to some. Bozena was petite and pretty but a lightweight dancer and Jan gave her heaps. Some people just shine on stage, they have a pizzazz, a confidence and an appeal that your eyes go to immediately. That sort of panache usually comes as a result of knowing what you are doing in the first place. Bozena had her own brand of charm on stage but she enraged Jan because she had difficulty grasping the choreography and could never quite get the timing right. Livid and completely at the end of his tether, Jan targeted her in rehearsal one day. I was on the top stage one tier back for this section of the routine; Bron and Bozena were out front. We'd been going at it all afternoon. Everyone was tired and salty with sweat. We needed to shower and rest before the show that night but Jan was determined that Bozena was going to get this sequence exactly right. He was in a filthy mood and stormed about the room, arms waving. He stood back and made us go over and over and over it.

'Five . . . six . . . seven . . . eight . . . again,' he'd demand. 'Five . . . six . . . seven . . . eight . . . again,' and again and on and on it went.

The more Bozena stuffed up, the more he stuck his heels in. Everyone got cranky but he was resolute: we were going to stay there until Bozena got it. After the umpteenth time, he finally lost it completely and ripped into her. The rest of us had to stand by, witnessing her humiliation and degradation while he dished out scathing criticism. Finally, exhausted and totally over it, he threw his hands up in despair, signalled and called to me.

'Robyn, get down here will you? Swap places with Bozena!'

And that was the end of that.

We all lived in the same apartment block—Bron and I were roommates—and each night we climbed into a minibus that taxied us to and from La Cupola D'oro. Dinner was provided each evening accompanied by giant bottles of wine. We dined on delicious garlic and olive oil–drenched Italian cuisine but it wasn't long before management put all the girls on diets. The creamy pastas and crusty garlic breads were showing on our hips and thighs.

For this show I usually rehearsed in a black, high-necked, low-back leotard and tan-coloured leather cowboy boots, which were tight and difficult to get into. I had this brainwave idea of wearing plastic over my feet so I could ease in and out of them until I wore them in and the leather softened. During one of the rehearsals, it was just Pete and me on stage working on a pas de deux from the *Funny Girl* piece. The rest of the cast were sprawled about the auditorium looking on. I had an enormous headdress with a long train that we had to get comfortable with. We were practising a tricky lift, Jan giving us the direction. Pete had to hoist me straight up so I could plant my foot firmly on his shoulder; he would secure me with one hand at my thigh and the other at my ankle.

'Take off your boots, Rob,' he said. 'They're too heavy and cumbersome. I won't be able to get a strong grip.'

Because I'd been wearing the plastic, my feet had acquired a rancid odour so I was reluctant to take them off, but I knew I had to get rid of them if we were going to get the lift right. We took our preparation, Jan counted us in. Pete glided towards me, executing excellent technique, strength and style as always. He placed his grip firmly and confidently then hoisted me up as I stretched my leg and lifted my torso. Everyone watching froze momentarily as Pete found his centre, and swiftly projected me vertically into space so I stood tall with my foot placed right next to his face. We'd only just managed to find our point of balance up there when Pete abruptly let go of me. I hit the floor with an almighty thud as he gasped in disgust.

'What is that stench? Your feet bloody stink!' he bellowed, shaking his head and stomping around the stage, panting for air.

'I'm sorry. It's my boots, it's my boots,' I explained, red-faced and embarrassed.

Everyone else broke out into raucous laughter.

On our days off, Bron and I sometimes headed to Switzerland, only a few hours north by train. The scenery of picture-perfect hamlets dotting soaring mountains inspired our imaginations. Sometimes in the warm summer months, groups of us got together to picnic in Locarno or on the shores of Lake Como. We fed pigeons in the magnificent Piazza del Duomo and bought clothes from Fiorucci. In winter the towns were like magical wonderlands, hushed and peaceful, blanketed in snow. We drank strong coffee and ate rich chocolates in cosy, fire-warmed cafés, and at Christmas time the people from our local trattoria gave Bron and I panettone, a traditional Italian Christmas cake that we scoffed with champagne on Christmas Eve.

After the show each night everyone got together in someone's apartment or in a restaurant, where we had late suppers of simple local dishes and fresh seafood. These shindigs were loud and outrageously funny, mostly because of the gay men all vying to be the centre of attention, each trying to outdo the others with their wicked sense of humour or their individual renditions of

'Cabaret' or 'New York, New York'. It was when everyone let their hair down that friendships were forged, petty problems sorted and egos put into place.

Milan is home to La Scala, the most beautiful opera house in the world, and when stars of the Bolshoi Ballet were scheduled to perform there, Pete organised a group booking for a matinee show, which would allow enough time for all of us to get back in time for our own show. The performance was thrilling and the ambience inside the theatre mesmerising. but afterwards the foyer flooded with a tide of exiting patrons. Making our way out to the street, pushing and shoving broke out. People frantically jostled for cabs and somehow, Julia, one of the English dancers, and I became separated from the others.

We must have been near them but we couldn't, for the life us, see anyone familiar. Hordes of people were queued up for taxis, it began to rain and as dusk turned to evening we worried about getting back to work in time. We must have grabbed the eye of a driver because quite suddenly a cab pulled up right next to us. He flung the back door open and in we jumped.

'*La Cupola D'oro, La Cupola D'oro per favore, signore. Grazie, grazie,*' we stammered in our best Italian, relieved to be out of the chaos. The cabbie dodged pedestrians and weaved his way out of the congestion while we sat back to catch our breath.

Moments into our ride, I noticed there was a strange-looking fare device on the dashboard and it wasn't ticking over. I sat up to investigate. Then the driver took a turn off the main drag and I didn't recognise the surrounds at all. I sensed danger and darted my eyes all about hoping to spot a landmark, sculpture, fountain, bus stop, house, street, *anything* that was vaguely familiar, but there was nothing except a vast expanse of deserted parkland. My adrenalin began to kick in.

'Julia, does this look familiar to you? Are we on the right road?'

'Gosh, Rob, I don't know.' She too sat up and looked all about nervously.

'Hey, driver, where are we?' I called out. 'Driver, driver, where are we?' He turned his head away from the road and looked at me, seated in the back. As we drove under a dim yellow street light I was able to glimpse the smug expression on his face and knew right away this man was a creep and we were in trouble.

'Let us out, please, let us out!' I yelled but the bastard completely ignored me; he said nothing and just kept going.

'Shit, Julia, we're in trouble.'

'Rob, what are we going to do?' She started to sniffle while I was trying to concoct a plan to escape.

'Stop it, Julia. Don't panic!' I ordered. 'Now listen to me. We're going to have to jump.'

'We can't fucking do that,' she cried in her posh English accent.

'Yes we can, and we are going to have to, Julia, so stop your blubbering.'

Ahead I could see what looked like a small restaurant, lights in the distance, signs of life.

Robyn and her siblings.
From left to right (rear) Richard,
Frank (front) Cathy, Julie
and Robyn.

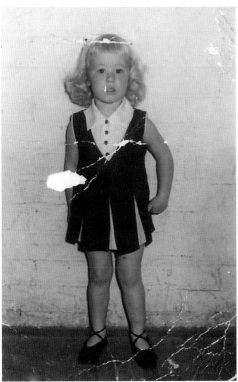

Robyn dressed for a physical
culture performance at the
Mosman Town Hall.

John and Shirley Windshuttle.

Gary and Robyn in front of the house that was towed up Gladstone Street. On the far right is the temporary dwelling.

In the change room of the Merry Minstrel show with Red Rob.

In Rehearsal

TAKING a break to pose for the camera before the beginning of rehearsals at the Opera House today were these members of the cast of the Merry Minstrel Show, performing in the city tonight and tomorrow night. From left: Carol Anderson, Peter Kaye (the leading man), Raymond Knock (one of the minstrel boys), Cheryl Hazelwood, Sula Cartier (the leading woman), Robyn Windshuttle and Alison Duncan.

A newspaper clipping about the Merry Minstrel Show with some of the cast: from left to right, Carol Anderson, Peter Kaye, Raymond Knock, Cheryl Hazelwood, Sula Cartier, Robyn and Alison Duncan.

Robyn with the Bluebells in the dressing rooms at the Palace Theatre, Excelsior Hotel, Hong Kong. The Bluebells are the internationally renowned dancers from the Lido in Paris.

La Cupola Doro, Milan. Jan Arntz (left), Eric (middle) and Robyn (far right).

Back stage at La Cupola Doro, Milan, with Djon.

An afternoon stroll in Paris with Dan and Danielito at
Les Jardin Des Tuilleries.

On the ferry from Barcelona to Ibiza.

Daniel and his brother Chiquito with Danielito.

In Ibiza. Even drug traffickers have promotional T-shirts.

On the beach at Celido on the New South Wales north coast. Daniel couldn't believe that such beaches existed with so few people.

Robyn and Danielito in Bogota, Colombia, on the way home to Europe.

Robyn still dancing after returning home to Australia permanently.

'Okay, Julia, get yourself together, listen to me and do exactly as I say. Don't hesitate; just do it. Grab the door handle and on the count of three lever it open and when I say jump you have to go for it, you have to jump. Okay? Are you ready?'

'Yes, Rob, yes. I'm ready.'

My mind raced furiously and I could feel the thud of my heart jumping in my chest. I took a deep breath and counted.

'One . . . two . . . three . . . Go, Julia, go,' I yelled. But just as I tried to pry the door open, my shirt sleeve hooked onto the door handle. I couldn't believe it. I fidgeted and clawed frantically. I was stuck and I couldn't free myself to open the door.

'I'm stuck, Julia. My sleeve is caught.'

'Oh fuck,' she cried.

Then, the driver, suddenly aware of our attempt to throw ourselves onto the road, slowed to a stop.

'Jump, Julia, jump, go . . . go!' I screamed. He turned to me again and this time reached out over the seat, extended a long arm and grabbed my boob, gripping it so hard it hurt. At once I knew that I was going to have to knock this guy out if we were going to survive this dilemma unscathed and I remembered the lesson I had been given by a martial arts enthusiast and friend of mine, Lee, back in Sydney not long before I took off: 'If you want to knock someone out, make sure your wrist is flat and in a straight line with your arm and elbow; aim, and shoot from your shoulder, that will deliver the power.'

After what seemed like an eternity but in reality was only a couple of moments, my sleeve came free. My aching boob still in the driver's grasp, I drew my elbow back, aligned my wrist and delivered an almighty blow to his forehead. I slammed him with all the force I could muster. He floundered, collapsed back into his seat, let out a gasp of pain and released his grip.

'Let's go, let's go,' I screamed to Julia, who was still only halfway out the door.

We fled as fast as we could, running for our lives towards the lights ahead and burst into the little café-bar puffing and panting, startling an elderly couple who were sitting quietly, having a drink. The barman—a short, rotund man with a moustache—glared at us like we were aliens. Except for the sound of a radio humming in the background, the place was eerily quiet and empty. Julia and I peered out the windows to see the man in the taxi drive past. Our jaws dropped open when we saw that the sign on the roof of his car didn't read 'Taxi' at all—we had been duped.

Eventually we got ourselves to work in a legitimate taxi to find a worried cast on the verge of calling the police. Still shaking from the whole ordeal, we got into costume, made up our faces and put on a smile. The show must go on!

೦೧

Seasons came and went but not a day passed without my thoughts turning to Daniel and the reunion I so eagerly awaited. I can hardly believe I held on for so long but I waited, patiently and steadfastly, for that day to arrive. Jan had ideas for a new production and tried talking me into signing up again but I refused; I knew from my communications with Jenny that Daniel's release was imminent but I had not anticipated just how soon I would be on my way.

It was the end of the week; we'd all piled onto the bus and were on our way to work. Everyone was subdued, which I assumed was because we'd partied hard the night before at my flat and our little shindig had ended in an ugly biffing match between Jan and Peter Pan. Jan had had too much to drink and suddenly became very aggressive. He scorned me for smoking dope and attacked my character. He was nasty and angry and tore into me in front of everyone. I was shocked and very hurt because I thought Jan had always liked me and had always been more than happy with my work. He'd tried so hard to convince me to stay on for the new production so I didn't understand this abrupt change in attitude. Pete had come to my aid; he'd stood up for me and was ready to flatten Jan. The rest of the cast looked on in horror but before things got really bloody, Jan's partner, Eric, hauled him off. After all that drama it was no wonder the atmosphere was tense that night on the bus but I sensed something more was up.

Sure enough, as we filed into La Cupola heading for the dressing rooms out back, Jan appeared from the front office and intercepted me.

'Robyn, come with me, please.'

Everyone else kept moving while I followed Jan into the office. Eric and Luigi, the head honcho who had financed the production at La Cupola, stood behind a desk glaring at me sternly like the Spanish Inquisition. Their intimidating presence was alarming and I knew something was definitely up. Then without warning the three of them bombarded me with a fusillade of accusations and criticism. They condemned me for smoking dope—drugs of any sort would not be tolerated in this company, not in Milan, not anywhere in Italy. They also condemned me for cavorting with Maximo, Luigi's son. The boss's son! I didn't even know Maximo was the boss's son. It was true he took a bit of a shine to me and we had shared a harmless joint. It was one time only though and, as far as I knew, he was just a humble stagehand. I'd smoked dope with an Italian DJ I'd met at a club, too, and ended up spending the night with him, but how would Jan know about that? He was furious with me, and though Eric tried to mediate, his loyalties were with his boyfriend, and Luigi, a right-wing, conservative Catholic, now despised me and just wanted me out. He was convinced that I had led his son astray and that I was a druggie. It was all very dramatic and way over the top. I really didn't get how big a deal it was until they told me I had to leave Milan, that my contract was cancelled, and that I had to get out of the country, *pronto*. Shit!

Someone had sabotaged me; how else would they know these personal details of my life? But I could only guess at who until the other dancers confirmed my suspicions. From the beginning, one

142

of the Dutch girls was after my place in the show. She hadn't been placed up front and centre by Jan because she wasn't good enough and that really pissed her off. She was jealous and although I sensed her resentment and caught the scowl on her face when she thought I wasn't looking, it never occurred to me that a person could be so downright dirty and manipulative. Knowing how Jan despised dope smoking, she had gone straight to him with the information and now I was out.

It was all very sudden and a bit of a shock to be out of a job and ordered to leave the country but I gathered myself together. After lots of hugs and teary goodbyes from most of the cast, Bron accompanied me to the train station the next evening. I had called Anne in Paris, who proved to be a reliable friend and had no trouble welcoming me into her home. What's more, she had some unbelievably heartening news: Daniel would be free in a matter of weeks.

Hovering on the platform, Bron and I shivered nervously, shifting our weight from one foot to the other, trying to ward off the chilly draught gusting from the tunnel. Overhead a call for passengers in French, English and Italian rang out. Commuters hurried past, porters pushed baggage carts, trains hissed and burped, and automated arrivals and departures alerts chimed. Sadness filled both of us as we embraced.

'Now stay in touch, Rob, won't you?' Bron said as we released our grip.

As the train pulled out slowly, I looked back to see my loyal friend waving furiously, smiling brightly until she disappeared out of sight.

I didn't catch up with Bron for another 30-odd years. Eventually she told me the Dutch girl who'd schemed against me never made it up front and centre despite her desperate attempts. The new production never got off the ground because Jan and Luigi had an almighty falling out over production costs. Jan chucked a hissy fit, packed up and left abruptly. The cast were not paid and had to make their own way out of the mess.

17

*A*nne and Guy had moved up in the world and were now living in a trendy new apartment one street back from Saint-Germain-des-Pres. To get to it I had to pass through a huge arched medieval-like, wooden door that opened in to a cobblestone courtyard. From Anne's apartment a narrow pathway led through a canopy of leaves to a meadow where a vacant, imperial-looking building, much like a small castle, gave way to gardens resplendent in early spring bloom. It was a gorgeous little oasis in the heart of Paris, a place of solitude marred only by the dim drone of traffic beyond the stone wall. A peeping chorus of sparrows flitted to and fro in the birdbaths while I lounged about on a soft carpet of lawn under a blue sky counting down the days until Daniel's release.

Soon I would be reunited with my lover; I could hardly believe it. Despite the exhilarating highs and miserable let downs and the almost life-threatening predicaments I'd got myself into I'd done well, I thought. I had managed to score good work and I was proud of myself for being able to rely on my talent. Soon, after all this time, I would be in Daniel's fond embrace again. I had imagined it, visualised it and longed for it. I had poured out my feelings onto paper. My poetry had become the friend I so desperately needed to talk to, but as our reunion drew closer a little doubt grew. I wavered between excitement and apprehension and that surprised me. My belief in this thing I had with Daniel had sustained me but now, poised on the verge of plunging back in with him, I wasn't sure if it was what I actually wanted. Had it been an illusion of my own making? Was this real love or had it been just a fantasy?

In Amsterdam, I had phoned my mother, reversing the charges, to ask for money and had to explain why I was in such dire circumstances. Luckily she had some money saved, hard-earned money, to send me but she was worried and when I convinced her everything was fine she then became annoyed about having to give up her savings. I couldn't possibly tell her the real circum-stances; what would she say if she knew the truth? Of course she would disapprove of Daniel and the life he had led me into but I didn't want to alarm her unnecessarily. I probably needed a family member to question my choices and to remind me of who I was and where I came from but I refrained from opening up. Although I kept in touch with my mother our communication was infrequent and each time we spoke I felt a growing distance between home and the life I was now living. I wanted to talk to her about my doubts but because we had grown so far apart I didn't want to trust her with my feelings.

I quickly realised I had to see Daniel again if only to discover whether this love we shared was a big sham. On the night of his release I was to meet him at La Coupole for dinner along with his lawyer and a few others, who I can only vaguely remember. La Coupole is a brasserie in the fourteenth arrondisement in Montparnasse, and in its heyday was a popular rendezvous point for the artistic intelligentsia. It's a huge, busy room with high ceilings and wooden cubicles, ornate mirrors and Art Deco murals on the walls. You practically drown in the ambience of La Coupole as you walk in. I was nervous that night. The memory of Daniel rose up in my chest and my cheeks flushed as I looked around furtively. Waiters bustled about in their black and whites, noisy dinner chatter bounced off the walls and then I saw him. As I approached, the whole table respectfully stood to greet me. It felt as if everything was in slow motion and the din of the restaurant hushed as Daniel and I looked at each other. Everyone at the table waited, frozen momentarily in an awkward silence but then he stepped forwards, took me in his arms and planted a passionate kiss on my lips.

'Hi, my love.' He grinned. 'My angel, you are beautiful, *qué linda*. Come, sit with me, my baby.'

The conversation returned to where it had broken off at my arrival. Dinner was served while I sat silently by his side with my hand clutched in his under the table. Effortlessly and readily, we picked up the thread of our love as if not one day had passed. He was just as I remembered, charming, engaging and commanding. I was so happy to be next to him again. My sense of relief was enormous.

We lived on Rue du Cotentin for a while, above a noisy Algerian grocer's store. The apartment was old and musty, sparsely furnished with a bed, couch, table and rudimentary kitchen; a bit of a dump really. Each time I sat on the loo, an icy cold draught swept up, shooting a chill straight through me. It was no palace but it would do for a while, until Daniel crawled back to respectability.

That first night at home in 'The Happy House' as we called it, we were initially reserved, polite with each other, stealing glances, that is until he took my hands in his and pulled me to his raging heart, kissing my fingers. His arm slid to my waist, tracing the contour of my back up to my neck and we came together, me clinging to his chest, he ruffling my hair, breathing in my scent. Laying me back onto the bed he pressed into me, his hardness leaping up. I watched him watching me, and saw his joy. Groaning with desire he filled me with pleasure until finally, with a fury I had never known before, he finished. Lying peacefully entwined in each other's arms we drifted into slumber.

We lived modestly, dining on fifteen franc steak frites dinners in cheap restaurants in Montparnasse or on hearty French fare at Aux Artistes just down the road, which was always crowded and noisy with local artists engaged in lively discussions about their works, which were displayed on the walls. Breakfast was ham omelettes in a brasserie across from our apartment. The proprietor there was an effeminate, balding man with a paunch and a miserable spirit. He whined his replies and took our orders begrudgingly. 'Ouiii d'accorrrd,' he sighed. He reeked of martyrdom, making it impossible not to laugh at him. Daniel thought he was a real prick, and deliberately antagonised him by mimicking his tone of voice and manner. To stir even further Daniel grooved into the brasserie one afternoon carrying an iridescent plastic beat box blasting away at full volume, with a comb-over hairdo so he looked like an absolute deadbeat. Other patrons couldn't help but notice and mostly got the joke and I found it amusing too, but not the proprietor; it only made him angrier.

Other times, after standing on the sidewalk for ages, trying to hail a cab down, Daniel's frustration with their refusal to even acknowledge us got the better of him. Striding out into the middle of the road he would plant his legs firmly apart and bring manic traffic to a screeching halt as he raised his hand to make a stop signal and yelled out, 'Stop, you fucking frog.' It always worked.

While Daniel was busy reestablishing clientele, I did classes in the dance studios in Clichy. That's where all the professionals went and where I would hear about any work prospects. There,

I ran into Zac, the African-American man I met that first day in Paris at Jenny's apartment. He offered me some teaching work in his studios in Saint-Germain-des-Pres and he was looking for a choreographer for a little job in the Caribbean for two weeks, which he thought I might like to take on. He had the dancers all lined up and I had his studios in which to rehearse. An easy two weeks on the shores of the Caribbean sounded ideal to me so I threw myself into the work with two African-American girls, a West Indian girl, a French girl and an English girl.

Guadeloupe is a group of tiny French islands just near the Bahamas. It's one of those picture postcard destinations with aqua waters, pristine beaches, palm trees and coral reefs. I was delighted to be visiting this exotic location and pleased to have the opportunity to choreograph. We performed our shows in packed town halls and community centres and a big rowdy restaurant-pub venue in the main town. The second week we flew across the Dominica Channel to Martinique. I dreaded that flight; small propeller aircraft always made me sick and nervous so I made sure I was first in and took shotgun in the cock pit next to the pilot for the 20-minute flight. It was in mountainous, lushly forested Martinique I met Roland.

He spotted me one night after the show and invited me out for lunch. Roland was born in the West Indies but these days he lived in Quebec, where he ran a nightclub and restaurant. His skin was the colour of ebony; he had a chubby, round face, big white teeth and short, black hair. I accepted his invitation but I didn't want to spend time with him alone so I made sure one of the other girls, Mary-Jo, came along too. We tasted authentic Creole dishes, rummaged for artefacts at the local markets and drank cocktails in a seaside eatery while being entertained by the chime of West Indian drummers.

Roland went all out to impress me but I wasn't quite sure what he wanted. I made it perfectly clear I wasn't interested in anything physical, that I would be returning to my lover in Paris any day, yet he kept on. At the end of the two weeks it all became clear: Roland had a proposition for me. He was looking for a dancer and a choreographer for his club back in Canada and invited me to come up and check it out, all expenses paid, including a return airfare.

This was a pretty big offer, I thought—and Canada no less! Now there is a destination. Still, I hardly knew this guy and I didn't think I would actually take him up on his offer but a couple of weeks after my return to Paris and after lengthy discussion with Daniel, I was on my way to French-speaking Quebec. I was nervous for sure, but Daniel was very reassuring and encouraged me to go, telling me it was a great opportunity. I wasn't so sure but talked myself into it. I was just going to check it out, after all. I didn't have to commit to anything and I could be back in Paris in a few days if things went awry. Still, I wasn't completely at ease with my decision and had to beat back my apprehension.

☙❧

The plane touched down early evening and as soon as I entered customs I could see Roland waiting for me at arrivals high up in the gallery area. Suddenly I wondered what the hell I was doing there surrounded by strangers, tired, a long way from home in unfamiliar territory and unsure about my fate with a stranger named Roland. My eyes brimmed with tears and I had a pressing urge to turn straight around and go home immediately.

Most of the passengers went through customs without a hitch but for me there was some problem: a customs officer led me off into an interrogation room, sat me down and proceeded to drill me about the nature of my visit. He was a pleasant fellow, calm and respectful, with a kind face. He was concerned that Roland was up to something devious and he was worried that I may find myself in trouble. After an interminable amount of time of him milking me for as much information as he could, he gave me a card with his details and told me to contact him if I found myself in trouble. I thought this unlikely.

Eventually Roland was called in and after more discussion between Roland and the customs officer, out of earshot I was led through. I could tell the kindly customs man was not happy by the way he eyed Roland sceptically as he escorted me out.

I'd only been in Quebec one day when I realised something was up. Roland had showed me around town and to his club, a New Orleans southern-style place with wide verandas. Then he'd put me up in a motel in the outskirts of the city and left me there for hours. When he did finally turn up with food and supplies he sleazily came on to me and was mortally offended when I turned him down. He assumed my refusal to have sex with him meant I was a lesbian. When I quizzed him about his real motives for luring me all this way, to my horror he disclosed his plans for me to star at his club doing strip tease.

At first I got angry: with myself for my stupidity at trekking off to Timbuktu to meet a complete stranger and with Daniel for not discouraging me in the first place. But my survival instinct kicked in and for my own safety I pretended to go along with Roland's plan, listening attentively to him and faking my interest. I knew I had to get out of this place so I deliberately hid my true feelings in order to buy myself some time. Once he left I pounced on the phone and tried to call Daniel but was aghast to discover I was unable to make any international calls; Roland had obviously anticipated my move and put a block in place. An agonising mix of panic and terror filled me before I remembered the customs guy. I had to get out of here and he was my only hope. It was late, dark outside already; there was a chance he wouldn't be in the office.

To my great relief he took my call and I hurriedly explained my dilemma. I told him of Roland's intentions to make me strip, how I had no return ticket, and how I couldn't call international because of a block on the phone. My voice quivered but I didn't dare entertain the possibility he wasn't going to help me. At first he sounded sceptical, then indifferent, so I pleaded with him, begged him to understand; then he got angry with me.

'You are a very foolish girl to have got yourself caught up with this dubious character,' he scolded.

Feeling stupid and desperate and overcome with stress, I started to cry, at which point pity must have overtaken him because he let out a huge sigh.

'Okay, okay, I'll see what I can do.'

He told me to get myself to the airport first thing the following morning and he'd sort something out. I had absolutely no choice but to trust him. So trust him I did.

At dawn I snuck out of the motel as quietly and secretively as a cat. I was petrified that Roland would suddenly turn up as I made my escape or the owners of the motel would see me and alert him. The area was quiet, isolated and remote, with dense native bushland all around. I had to hitchhike to the airport, which thankfully was heavily signposted on the highway otherwise I wouldn't have had a clue which direction to take. I pushed back panic and thought about my mum and wondered who would even know I was here if something bad happened.

I waited and waited, occasionally walking some distance before stopping again to look anxiously for an approaching car. The dawn light gradually lifted into an overcast sky and by and by I heard the throaty roar of an engine in the distance. I squinted and made out a white Corvette. Despite the gravity of my situation I couldn't help but give a tiny smile; not a bad car to materialise for a damsel in distress! The driver spotted me and cruised to a halt. I bent down to peer into the car through the passenger seat window so I could see his face. He was middle-aged with an air of mid-life crisis: he wore a tan suede jacket, blue jeans and cowboy boots. His command of English was about equal to my French, but I was able to convey fairly efficiently that I was headed to the airport. While I wasn't sure about him (he could have been a mass murderer for all I knew) I jumped in. The engine hummed as we drove on.

I sat demurely, nervous as hell, looking straight ahead and making as little conversation as possible. I just wanted to get to that airport, to be among people and feel safe. Occasionally he glared at me from the driver's seat, then he spoke to me, something about lunch. I agreed to *déjeuner* with him just to keep him happy until we got to the airport, but as soon as we arrived and slowed down in the car park I thanked him, leapt from the car and bolted into the terminal.

The customs man ushered me into his office and extracted all the sordid details of my stay in Quebec and how I got myself into this mess in the first place. My disclosure was more like a short history of my life. I tried calling Daniel several times throughout the morning, but there was no answer. I had to sign documents swearing to my statement, then the official told me that deportation was the only thing he could do for me. Deportation! I couldn't believe it. I wanted to return to Paris not Australia and the last thing I needed was a big red DEPORTED stamp in my passport.

He smiled. 'Don't fret. We'll fly you back to Paris, to your boyfriend, if that's where you want to go, and we will not stamp your passport either.'

With a gush of relief I gathered my baggage and headed for departures. I'll never know what became of Roland and I don't care, but I will never forget the customs man at Quebec Airport for his generous spirit and kindness.

18

*T*hat ordeal really rattled me. I got over it though and eventually the whole sordid episode melted into a distant memory. There was no point dwelling on it; besides, Daniel had found us a new place to live. We were moving on and out of Rue du Cotentin into a modern apartment in a chic part of town. He'd burst into the living room full of zeal and all smiles, his lanky frame bouncing as he strode in.

'Robs, Robs, my love, I have found our new palace. You are going to love it, my angel. Let's go, my baby. Let's move out of this dump.'

From there we lived like rock stars: zooming around in prestige cars, shopping at haute couture boutiques, dining in exclusive restaurants and partying all night at fashionable nightclubs. Upon our arrival the doormen, the cloak girls and usually the proprietor would flap around in a flurry of fervent handshakes and cheek kissing. Daniel would tip everyone and in we'd go. The best table in the house and a bottle of champagne would suddenly materialise. It was all so glamorous and exhilarating. My life with Daniel was a tremendous ride of joy, contentment and wonderful highs. This was the passionate love I'd always dreamt of and Daniel was the man I knew I would be connected to forever.

When we first met I thought his camera was his main source of income—he'd done a few exhibitions and I'd seen his impressive work so I had no reason to think otherwise—but this new life showed me the truth. Daniel, like lots of Colombian nationals, was making extraordinary sums of money through the distribution of Colombia's biggest export, and our lifestyle reflected that. Good cocaine is like French champagne. It is a stimulant but it is subtle and the exultant high from cocaine does not hit you like a sledge hammer; rather it creeps up on you and catches you unawares later, and in the seventies it was the party drug for the elite. We kept the company of high-profile lawyers, Swiss bankers, realtors, actors, painters, models and photographers. There was nothing remotely boring or dull about our lives. Everyone wanted cocaine, and Daniel and his Colombian compadres had the goods. *Perico* was easy money that came from the *fincas* in the mountains of Colombia where poor farmers were paid heaps of money to work fields of coca leaves.

There was a whole crew of Colombians living in Paris and we became close in a familial way, because our working, family and social lives spilled over into each other's on a daily basis. If we didn't go clubbing we'd meet up for dinner or attend little soirees at someone's apartment. One friend—Fernando—was called Pluma Blanca because his full head of dark, wavy hair had a white, feather-shaped streak through it. He and his wife, Gina, lived in an apartment just near the Eiffel Tower with their young daughter. There was another Fernando, who looked more like a North American Indian. He was tall and extremely good looking and reminded me of Wind in his Hair from *Dances with Wolves*. One woman I met, Yvonne, lived like a movie star, flying back and forth between Bogotá and Paris and other breathtaking locations, always dressed in up-to-the-minute fashion. She was mistress to some big shot drug lord back in Colombia and I didn't like her icy, too-cool-to-be-true manner. She never missed an opportunity to belittle me—she thought we Australians were parochial. She was a snob and foolishly believed in her own exaggerated self-importance.

Javier, the intellectual, a political journalist and correspondent for Colombia press, lived and worked in Paris with his wife and their two sons. We often saw Javier on current affairs programs discussing politics foreign affairs and other important global matters with prominent heads of state. He was embroiled in a steamy affair with a blonde-haired Colombian girl who studied at la Sorbonne. She possessed a sophisticated intellect and avariciously pursued wealthy older men. She also spoke fluent French and Italian and her best friend, Veronique, a stern French girl who lived in Trocadero, was editor of a fashionable woman's magazine. Eva, a pretty Swedish woman, ran a model agency in Paris and New York and her boyfriend, George, a flirty charmer, spoke in a deep, sexy voice that he amped up in the presence of attractive women. Eva introduced us to Pete, a big tall blonde guy, who got his start on Fleet Street and now travelled all over the world photographing celebrities and models. He always managed to put himself in the right place at the right time so as to capture highly sought-after images the media paid heavily for. Pete was British but had spent most of his life in Australia. His affinity with Australia and fondness for the lifestyle bonded us imme-diately; we shared an understanding of space and distance on a scale unimaginable to our city-dweller friends. His friendship was a welcome relief from the intensity of the South Americans and the seriousness of the French.

Guillermo, a funny little man with a wicked sense of humour, fought incessantly to please his cranky red-headed wife, Rosario; nothing was ever good enough for her. Luis was the tight-arse and the target of regular jokes because of his stinginess and Angelique, his tall, elegant girlfriend from Brazil, had been educated in the United States. Circqoo, a stunning platinum-blonde Finnish model, had guys drooling at the very sight of her. She loved the Brazilian Carlos, but I thought he was a bludger and pimp the way he leeched off her. Chencho, a tubby man with a big balding head, laughed and spoke like the cartoon character Elmer Fudd, and Adrianne, the air hostess, walked on and off planes with luggage brimming with contraband all the way from Colombia.

The men referred to their compadres as *flaco* if they were thin and *gordo* if they were fat and used *cabron*—'mate'—as a term of endearment. Out of earshot of the women, the men congregated to discuss business, always in the soft dialect of Colombian Spanish, while maids prepared delicious South American dishes and we women lounged about looking glamorous. With business all wrapped up, the mood lightened and we'd gather around a huge dining table and eat heartily. After dinner a small mountain of coke was emptied onto a glass surface, the music was turned up and the party continued. This is what Colombians did. And everyone danced, including the men. I was impressed by that. They had an innate sense of rhythm, and were gregarious, high-spirited, passionate people who loved to salsa. For them, life was one big rhumba.

The Colombians nicknamed the straight, conservative types who partied hard on coke from Friday to Sunday 'weekend warriors'. We got invites to art shows, photographic exhibitions, embassy gatherings and film premieres and sometimes to the after-parties of high-profile entertainers currently in Paris. I was often starstruck, brushing shoulders with all the big celebrities of the time.

It was usually the early hours of the morning before we emerged from our all-night carousing. Paris was magnificent in the dawn light. Dirty streets littered with steaming dog poo and rubbish and the decadence that throbs just under the surface of Parisian life were camouflaged in a soft violet hue. The hush of the city, the elegance of Pont Alexandre III—its Art Nouveau lamps, cherubs and nymphs—and the Seine winding its way through the heart of Paris were arrestingly beautiful at that time of day.

On the surface, the Colombian crew were suave and sophisticated. They were polite and came across as cultured and educated. Daniel, though, reminded me constantly not to trust them. I was to be careful about what I said and who I spoke to. He warned me not to be deceived by their charm, claiming they would do anything to lure me away from him.

'Colombians,' he told me, 'are a ruthless bunch of thugs, Robs. They don't give a shit. They are savages.'

In time I would see that their hunger for affluence and their façade of respectability was rooted in the corruption and violence rife in Colombia, where ostentatious wealth lives side by side with abject poverty. Daniel, like all the Colombian crew, was gripped by the staggering amount of cash that could be made from the humble coca leaf. The Colombians have this amazing constitution for cocaine and could party on it for hours, even days, a throwback perhaps to their primitive Indian cultures when it was used for medicinal purposes and to relieve altitude sickness.

The more I became entrenched in this unconventional lifestyle, the more I became entwined with Daniel, our connection deepening and intensifying. He became the most significant person in my life and, ensconced in his custodial grip, I thought our zestful, flashy life and his tenderness and loving affection were everything I wanted. He made me feel loved, as if I were the only person that mattered to him. When he looked at me he peered into my soul and when he smiled at me my heart shone. In reality, we were balanced precariously on a fine line between stability and chaos, but I couldn't see that. I had become an accomplice to the illicit dealings of a bunch of cocaine cowboys.

19

*D*oris Haug was the head honcho at the Moulin Rouge. The dancers at the Moulin, the Doris Girls, were her charge and through my friend Ruud I heard she was looking for someone. Ruud had relocated to Paris while I was in Milan and it was he who encouraged me to get in touch with her.

Doris lived in Montmartre, on the highest hill in Paris just up behind the Moulin Rouge, and to get to her place I had to make an arduous climb up hundreds of century-old steps from Boulevard de Clichy, in Pigalle, the red light district of Paris. Pigalle earned its raunchy reputation in World War Two from Allied soldiers—who called it pig alley—and was filled with an eclectic mix of tourists, street girls, pimps, addicts, illegal immigrants, artists and musicians. It was, for me, the most unlikely address for the Moulin Rouge, but smack bang in the middle of all this crud there it stands, its iconic red windmill imposing and oddly sassy. At the top of the steps is the beautiful la Basilique du Sacré-Coeur, the white-domed basilica, standing supreme overlooking all of Paris. I made my way through gardens, past old houses, up steep streets and across Place du Tertre, a village square and renowned artistic locale for Toulouse-Lautrec, Pablo Picasso, Claude Monet and Vincent Van Gogh.

I had to enter Doris's lofty apartment by a mossy terraced garden overgrown with ivy, shrubs and vines. Inside, it was cosy and dishevelled in a comfortable, lived-in way. Black and white photos of Doris in her heyday hung above a piano placed next to a massive bookshelf crowded and overflowing with all manner of literature. Grand windows showed sweeping views of the city encompassing the Boulevard de'Etoile, the Arc de Triomphe, the Eiffel Tower and the Seine.

I liked Doris the moment I met her. She was direct, honest and down to earth. Some would say she was abrupt, but I related to that easily. A statuesque woman, Doris, like most choreographers in Europe, appreciated Australian dancers. We were a 'disciplined lot', she said; we possessed 'character and strength and style'.

'Show me your walk, Robyn, up and down the room,' she demanded. Knowing how to walk is an art form and, aside from a strong classical technique, the clincher to being hired. She sat there with an unremarkable expression on her face as I glided back and forth. Within moments she saw I had the necessary poise and grace and abruptly ended the audition for a more relaxed, friendly chat.

Our meeting was short and sweet and then Doris instructed me to be at Le Moulin for rehearsals the next morning for the real audition.

Most people know of Le Moulin because of the legendary can-can, immortalised by the painter Toulouse-Lautrec. First appearing in the 1830s, dancers would perform high kicks energetically and provocatively, lifting their dresses and revealing their legs and underwear. It occasionally caused public outrage with claims it was too erotic or vulgar. At its peak in the late nineteenth century, the can-can was the dance adopted by courtesans to attract male clientele. Later, when music hall entertainment became increasingly popular all over Europe, le Moulin Rouge became a legitimate nightclub, without the courtesans. With Doris Haug and Ruggero Angeletti at the helm, the modern can-can evolved and a dazzling new review opened, attracting beautiful and leggy ballet dancers with exceptional skill who hadn't made it into traditional companies.

Le Moulin Rouge has a reputation as the most famous cabaret in the world and over the years has attracted notable performers, such as Liza Minnelli, Frank Sinatra, Maurice Chevalier, Ella Fitzgerald, Edith Piaf, Sacha Distel and Charles Aznavour. *The Ed Sullivan Show* was taped from le Bal du Moulin Rouge in 1962 and several movies have been made about it. Fabulous stage settings, original music scores, feathers, rhinestones, sequins and some say the most beautiful girls in the world grace its stage.

As arranged, I turned up for rehearsal next morning, coming through the front entrance, into the lights and the sound of music and dancers' feet up on stage. I remember a huge tiered auditorium with blue velvet furnishings and chandeliers. The dance captain was putting everyone through their paces. The star of the show was a glamorous West Indian entertainer. At the top of the hierarchy of sixty-odd dancers were two soloists, one of them a South Australian girl, then six dancers, of whom I was to be one—hopefully—and then the corps of male and female dancers. Doris sat out front along with a pride of officialdom who scrutinised me as I shook their hands. I walked on stage, took my place and proceeded to follow the captain's lead. I was the only one auditioning so I relaxed into it, aware of the energy of the other dancers around me. The choreography came to me easily, so I moved with confidence and let my heart dance. As I spun and glided and lunged and lifted I caught a glimpse of Doris's face and could see from her expression she was pleased.

Costume fittings were arranged, including for the wigs and headdresses I'd need. I had to buy some new dance shoes, makeup and G-strings. I slotted in comfortably without a hitch and it was great to be working again. I always felt so in my own skin dancing on stage—it was where I belonged. Besides, the lustre of the racy lifestyle with Daniel was wearing off. I was growing restless and bored with our idle days and late party nights; I needed some balance in my life and yearned to get busy again with meaningful activity, to get my teeth into something productive, and a place at the Moulin Rouge would do nicely.

The Moulin was a full house every night. Hundreds of tourists from all over the world took their seats while backstage the routine of makeup, hair, warmup, half-hour call, five-minute call, lights, orchestra, then show time played out. On cue we presented on stage. We moved stealthily from the dark shadows in the wings to greet the audience. Bathed in strong beams of light, I moved languidly and gracefully across the stage; confident, smiling, happy. We had some lyrical dance sequences to perform and a contemporary tribal piece with headdresses adorned with stunning feathers. Awash with spectacular plumage, diamantes and exotic costumes, the dancers transformed the stage into a collage of colour and movement. It lit up with the energetic can-can and the provocative low-cut bodices above full can-can skirts supported by lacy petticoats.

After the exhilarating dance sequences we'd dash about making costume changes in supersonic time, flying up and down rickety stairs, always over a chorus of excited babble and laughter. Onstage again, rows of leggy dancers descended a staircase past beautifully shaped nudes draped elegantly with rhinestone necklaces, while handsome male dancers coasted around us. World-class singers, acrobats and magicians appeared at le Moulin, a mock elephant, gaily adorned for a Middle Eastern production number, swaggered across the stage and—with the benefit of modern hydraulics and massive sets—a swimming pool miraculously materialised from the guts of the theatre to reveal a mermaid swimming with a sea snake. The audiences were always mesmerised, their applause intoxicating. It was thrilling, exciting and I felt so proud to be there.

Most of the expat dancers rented accommodation close to Le Moulin in impossibly tiny studios that cost the earth. There were a couple of sisters from New Zealand, some Australians and lots of British girls and boys. We'd catch up and chat about our lives and swap the latest gossip in between costume changes or waiting in the wings: who was sleeping with whom; who was going to be axed; what work was in the wind. But I rarely socialised with my dance friends outside of work because Daniel was the focus of my life. Of an evening he'd zoom me to work in his flashy BMW then usually meet me after the show for a late supper before we headed off into the night. There was always a party somewhere and new friends, a trendier club, a fancier restaurant. Wherever there was cocaine there were the wealthy, the chic, the artistic, the models, and Daniel was at the centre, vibrant, charming, engaging. Usually it would be close to dawn before we finally slid into bed, aroused by the charge of cocaine. Our desire for each other was insatiable, our erotic play steamy, lascivious and sensual. Lustful pleasure and intimacy consumed us.

I savoured the subdued times too; usually when we had outdone ourselves in the night scene we'd restore our souls with a quiet stroll along the Seine, a movie or a wander up narrow laneways into obscure book stores, galleries and gardens. The Bee Gees' new album *Saturday Night Fever* was playing in all the nightclubs and we couldn't get enough of it. 'How Deep is Your Love?' still resonates with me 30-odd years later, as does the Bellamy Brothers' 'Let Your Love Flow'. Occasionally I'll hear them play and am immediately transported back to the time when Daniel and I were immersed in a blazing romance.

But nothing ever stays the same. I had learned early on that change is inevitable and had adopted a philosophical approach to the shifts and turns of life; it was a coping mechanism of sorts. I loved the growth, the renewed energy and the reawakened passion that followed the rearrangement of our daily lives but those rewards sometimes came at the price of pain, uncertainty and broken trust; I dreaded that side of it. And I heard it in Daniel's voice one night as I was getting ready for work. He called from the other room.

'My love, tonight you will have to get a cab home. I will be caught up in business so I will see you later on.'

As soon as I heard those words something clinked in my heart—something was up. I pushed back the panic grumbling in my stomach. I was immediately suspicious and wondered what he was really going to be getting up to and with whom. I'd seen him flirting with other women but I dared not entertain the thought that he was actually fooling around with them. I stopped packing my work things and looked over as he entered the room to give me some francs. As I took the money he saw the worry on my face and scooped me up in his arms. He laughed and reassured me I had nothing to worry about, that I was just being paranoid. I felt embarrassed about my childish response and decided to trust him; it was up to me to deal with my feelings of insecurity.

His occasional late-night rendezvous without me, however, soon became a habit and a source of anxiety for me. I wasn't sure if my initial misgivings had been justified or if I was being irrational but I began to resent it when he couldn't pick me up, and the disappointment I felt when he didn't turn up at all without warning was sickening. As soon as the finale was over I'd fly up the stairs to remove the heavy stage makeup, hit the showers and dash out excitedly to meet him, only to find he was not waiting for me. I'd hang around for a few minutes, nervously looking up and down the boulevard, hoping he was just running late. Eventually, scared of hanging about alone on the streets of Pigalle amid a sea of seedy night people, I gave up and went home.

Even worse were the times when he picked me up, took me to dinner somewhere, smothering me with affection and 'baby this' and 'angel that', then ambushed me with his plan to drop me off home before choofing off into the night again without me. I never had a moment even to protest; it all happened so swiftly. I didn't understand; it felt like rejection. I wanted him to come home with me and wondered why he'd started to exclude me but somehow he always managed to convince me that it was best for me to stay snug at home, out of harm's way. I wanted to believe him but my instincts told me differently.

I began to spend more and more time in my own company. Doubts about his fidelity started to gnaw away in my head. I felt powerless. I had a sinking feeling that something precious was slipping away and there was nothing I could do to stop it. I took to talking to myself, trying to sort out my confusion; trying to convince myself that I was imagining it all; that somehow it was my fault and my responsibility. Punishing myself came too easily and, in retrospect, I should have trusted my instincts. Instead I buckled and handed him the power to manipulate me.

I usually passed the time by immersing myself in a book before falling asleep. Some nights he wouldn't return until dawn and there were spells when he'd keep me waiting for days before I saw him again. I'd lie awake, listening for the sound of his car or a cab idling on the street below. I slept fitfully, tossing and turning, hoping he'd walk in the door. It was tortuous, one ear always cocked, or worse, waking up scared with my heart in my throat. When finally he did walk through the door, smelling of the night, of other women, of Camel *sans filtre*, he was so adept at sweet talking me—and I so relieved to see him—I forgot about being angry all together. He was a very smooth operator.

Reluctantly, I accepted his rationale. I told myself, 'I can handle this. He loves me.' Foolishly I allowed myself to be wounded and forgave him every time. I thought he would see and appreciate how much love it took to endure him. Unable to confront the truth of what was unfolding, I excused him.

20

One night, Doris approached me back stage with an offer of a job in Tokyo for three months. Doris seemed to always be in tune with her dancers and I'm pretty sure she suspected something was up with me because I was distracted and undecided about signing up for the new production at the Moulin. Rehearsals for a new, bigger and better show were soon to begin but, with things as they were between Daniel and me, the timing of Doris's offer seemed right for me to take a break. Besides, Japan wasn't that far from Australia and I entertained thoughts about possibly flying home from there. So I accepted. We were only a small production and I was glad for that. We'd knocked over the rehearsals easily and left Paris quickly. I was afraid of leaving Daniel behind but I needed this break from him and the crazy life we were living so I embraced my decision.

Just before I left for Tokyo, Daniel suddenly swung back to devoted lover mode. The realisation that I was actually leaving hit him at the last minute, I think, and because I was emotionally vulnerable to him I lapped it up. Even though it was what my heart had ached for, I almost wished he hadn't changed, for it was all I needed to convince myself that our ailing connection had perhaps been all in my mind after all.

It was 1977 and the Golden Gessica restaurant and night-club in Tokyo was presenting the Doris Girls all the way from the Moulin Rouge in Paris. It was a popular cabaret located in Ginza, the most exclusive and expensive shopping area in Japan. Backstage in the dressing room a whole wall was devoted to autographs, messages and countries of origin from dancers and entertainers who had performed here over the years. In the maze of scribbles I recognised familiar names of friends and peers from Sydney and duly carved my own name, 'Newport Beach, Sydney', the date and 'Doris Girls from le Moulin Rouge'.

Tokyo was a vast, fascinating city, teeming with people and congestion. The pagodas, temples and shrines coexisted with a hyper-urban metropolis and conspicuous consumption unlike any city I had experienced before. This had once been the turf of shōgun, feudal law and samurai; now throngs of tech-savvy Tokyo-ites trotted to subways past neon signs, shiny architectural facades, designer boutiques, department stores and restaurants. I felt truly alien in this world of mountainous islands, raw fish, Zen Buddhism and cherry blossoms. In Tokyo, communication baffled me. No one was rude or dismissive, and greetings were respectful. I never quite knew if I was understood despite the curt nodding, humble bowing and practiced smiling. There were so many formal social customs and rituals. And I couldn't get used to the food. I quickly grew tired of a diet of sashimi, sushi, miso soup and green tea; it left me hungry and craving for a juicy rump steak, which was unbelievably expensive in Tokyo.

We stayed in a boutique hotel with tiny bathrooms. I shared a room with Katherine, a French girl with whom I could practise my French, and we did all the touristy things together. We explored the Meiji Shrine, dedicated to the deified spirits of Emperor Meiji and his consort Empress Shōken, and its surrounding forest. We immersed ourselves in the peace and beauty of traditional Japanese gardens with quaint bridges, running water, lilies, pebble pathways and bonsai. We had the good fortune to glimpse the spectacular beauty of a geisha in traditional costume and we witnessed young girls in their first kimono offering money at a Buddhist temple in exchange for a healthy, happy life. We trekked on foot up a steep mountainside decorated with streamers to attend a festival to see the elaborate costumes and makeup of kabuki, a stylised form of dance and drama, and bunraku, a traditional form of puppet theatre, and to hear the roar of taiko performers, Japanese drummers who, when we saw them, wore headbands and had heavily tattooed bodies.

My days and nights were consumed with thoughts of Daniel. I still hadn't decided if I was going home after this show or if

I was going back to Paris. I clutched at memories of him and anxiously waited for his phone calls, hoping to hear him affirm his love for me. I moped around, totally preoccupied with dreamy visions of this man and in the process robbed myself of properly experiencing Japan. But then Anne, my Danish friend from Paris, arrived. She was on her way to Australia and appeared at the stage door one night. I was so happy to see my friend again and we decided immediately to spend the next few days together sight seeing. We particularly wanted to see Mount Fuji, and the fastest way to get there was on the supersonic Bullet Train. On the train that day she filled me in with news of Daniel and all the gossip from Paris.

Anne knew I was troubled about Daniel's loyalty. She also knew he was no ideal partner but, like most people, she was drawn to his gregarious nature, his passionate heart and his charisma.

'You know, Robyn,' she said, 'Daniel misses you and I think he is expecting you to return to Paris after Tokyo. I know it can't be easy to be with him but some people wait all their lives for the sort of passion you share.'

Her words swam around in my head and only exacerbated my confusion. I'd always wanted to avoid an ordinary life and my relationship with Daniel had become an important element of the adventure I was living. I knew early on I didn't want a bland existence and deliberately sidestepped the straight, conventional route. A nice steady guy, marriage, a mortgage and three kids had never been on my agenda. But I wondered about the price

I was paying for passion and whether or not Daniel's love and lifestyle was going to drain too much from me.

Mount Fuji was breathtaking: a perfect cone-shaped volcano soaring into the sky shrouded in mist. Blanketed in pure white snow, it looked peaceful and serene. Anne and I jumped off the train at a remote village quite a distance from the circus of tourists at the foot of the mountain. It was sunny and bright but bone-chillingly cold as we ambled along a narrow road scanning the surrounds for signs of life. The area was deserted and eerily quiet except for bursts of wind rustling the leaves. Fuji stood majestic in the distance and the icy cold air stung our nostrils. We wandered on and further along as the road began to descend into a gully I spotted a little house perched high among the bushes.

'Come on,' I said to Anne, 'let's go and knock on the door.'

She was hesitant but I insisted and led the way up a path of stepping stones to a little pagoda-style cottage with tinkling wind chimes. We knocked, and waited for a short time, shivering in the cold, until a little old lady opened the door. She was wrapped in layers of clothing under a kimono and wore thick socks. She had a wrinkly brown face with a warm smile decorated with few teeth and had wispy grey hair pulled back into a bun. As she smiled, her whole face lit up and without hesitation she nodded and welcomed us into her home. We were complete strangers, obviously foreigners, but she had no compunction about inviting us in and led the way to her living room. She shuffled along, bowing her head, and then gestured for us to crouch on cushions around a low wooden table. A small open fire glowed in the corner. There were candles and fragrant incense burning and the chimes clanged furiously in a gust of wind, then stilled. We sat opposite her smiling and nodding, until she rose, bowed again and disappeared into another room. Anne and I sat silently, luxuriating in the tranquillity and serene spirit of the little old lady.

She returned some minutes later with a tray of steaming tea. We sipped the brew quietly with an occasional nod and smile to our host, whose weathered bright face nodded and smiled back. The silence was restorative, the ambience peaceful. No words were spoken between us but kindness and trust had bonded us in a brief and unexpected crossing of paths. Before Anne and I took our leave, we bowed humbly, grateful for this unforgettable encounter, one that could have been easily missed had we not ventured beyond the throngs of tourists. This sweet old lady with her generous spirit and kind smile left an indelible print in my mind, one that created a sense of hope and belief in even the slimmest of dreams.

On the train back to Tokyo I made my mind up to return to Paris. I wasn't ready to go home just yet.

21

The flight back to Paris was excruciatingly long and boring. We had to spend a night in Bangkok, which meant shuttling through oppressive humidity and an unbelievably crowded city. After three days of airports, I was glad to finally touch down at Charles de Gaulle Airport, excited but also anxious. I still wasn't sure I had made the right choice by coming back.

Night had fallen by the time my cab pulled up at our apartment. The air was chilly and steam vaporised from my mouth as I spoke. As the car idled I was scrounging around for some francs to pay the driver when Daniel suddenly appeared, bounding up to me in his leather bomber jacket with the fur collar.

'Robs, baby, my angel, you are here. Come, baby, come. How are you, my love?' he said with his trademark radiant smile, paying the driver and taking my bags.

That night the warmth of his familiarity seeped back into my soul, wrapping me in security. Daniel fussed over me with tender adoration and affection. He joked and laughed and hugged me so tightly it hurt. It didn't take long to settle back into our comfort zone. We were loved up and affectionate and any memory of hurt or pain was forgotten. We were back, stronger than ever. I was home again and I felt safe, reassured.

I dropped by the Moulin Rouge to sniff out work. I didn't necessarily want back into The Moulin, but I did want to find out through my friends there what work was on offer in town. As usual it was bigger than Ben Hur backstage. I passed by wardrobe to say hello and greeted the newer, younger dancers. I caught up with my Kiwi mates and paid my respects to Doris. Ruth, one of the five nudes I shared a dressing room with before Tokyo, had moved up the ranks to soloist next to the South Australian girl, who was in agony because her left nipple had been sliced on stage by a rhinestone. She was in tears and accusing Ruth of upstaging her and being responsible for her injury. They were engaged in a heated argument and had drawn quite a crowd. Ruth protested her innocence and, upon seeing me, seized my arm and dragged me into their dressing room, demanding I walk through the choreography as I remembered it—she needed me to prove her innocence. Thankfully I recalled the steps exactly and the dispute was settled. With Ruth's innocence confirmed the kerfuffle died down and gawking dancers dispersed to their respective change rooms.

Doris threw up her hands in dismay and I proceeded to milk the girls for information about the Crazy Horse. I recalled Jan Arntz in Milan having raved about it and there'd recently been a lot about it in the media. Doris shot me a reproachful glare.

'I hope you are not thinking of deserting to the Crazy Horse, Robyn Windshuttle.'

I hadn't made up my mind about it yet but when one of the dancers scoffed at the idea in a rather catty tone—'You won't get into the Crazy, Robyn. It is very selective'—my interest piqued immediately. Now, there was a challenge.

Three days after making contact with the Crazy Horse I was scheduled for an audition. Classical training was not a prerequisite for a place at the Crazy Horse and although most of the dancers had studied ballet there were quite a few who were just flat out gorgeous with only basic dance skills. The audition was impromptu with no choreography at all. I had to interpret the music and do my thing on a brightly lit stage. The house lights were down so I couldn't see who was in the audience. The dance captain cued me, the music played and I just started dancing. When it was all over I was summoned to one of the private change rooms where I was grilled by the boss about my work intentions and what I was doing in Paris. I wasn't entirely sure he was going to hire me but a few days later I got the call. Daniel and I were lying on the bed reading when the phone rang. He answered and then nervously handed me the phone.

'Robs, it's the Crazy Horse. It's the Crazy Horse, Robs.'

I think he was more excited than me. Rehearsal time was slotted in and off I went.

৩

The Crazy Horse Saloon was a chic, trendy cabaret located on Avenue George V. Its reputation for showing off sensual women with elegance and class attracted hordes of tourists, the rich and famous, rock stars, musicians, politicians and celebrities from all over the world. Patrons were led up a plush, carpeted hallway by doormen dressed in the uniform of the Royal Canadian Mounted Police, complete with hats made out of bear skin. The saloon was intimate with simple décor. The show was a provocative display of creative lighting and scantily clad women moving seductively about on a small stage miming to various songs. It was erotica but stunningly beautiful: the girls were sexy but not cheap; the choreography suggestive and daring but never blatant, trashy or vulgar. It was all class and it was packed every night. There are countless tacky copycat Crazy Horse shows all over the world but they cannot emulate the quality, elegance and style of the original. There is only one Crazy Horse.

At the time I worked there it was run by Alain Bernardin, a French entrepreneur who demanded all the girls adhere to his strict disciplinary code. Soft makeup, naturally styled hair, matte lips, no fraternising with guests. In my final rehearsal before my first show, I was whisked off to a hair salon in Saint-Germain-des-Pres where my waist-length sun-bleached tresses were transformed into a Farrah Fawcett–style layered cut. I was forlorn that I had to cut my hair but after several hours in the salon, I emerged with a soft, feminine cut that was far more elegant and sophisticated.

Dinner was provided for us from the restaurant next door. Bernardin didn't want us to go hungry and he didn't want us leaving the premises between shows. It was amusing observing the waiter enter the dressing rooms each night to take our orders while twenty or so half-naked women touched up lips, adjusted stockings, pulled on boots and rearranged wigs. Slightly embarrassed, not knowing quite where to look, he'd hand out menus and explain the specials of the day. One hour later our dinner arrived complete with silver service.

We wore full body makeup and each night before curtain Bernardin lined us up to give us the once over, just to make sure we maintained the classy image he wanted to emulate. He was a businessman, had resolved to keep the integrity and healthy reputation of his place intact, and he gave us all stage names. I was Rhoda Decorum, a fitting name bestowed upon me because I was a neat dancer, obviously classically trained and always mindful of the technique. There was Trucula, a pouty German, and Polly, an African-American and the dance captain. Goody, a beautiful French blonde, preferred girls and was booted out when Bernardin discovered she was working as an escort on the side. Regina, wife and mother of two and also Bernardin's lover from earlier days, was the oldest. Each night we'd entertain a spellbound audience with the beauty of our female forms. And Bernardin always had a car and a driver waiting at the end of each evening for anyone who didn't have a lift home and he personally wished all his girls a *bonsoir* at the doorway as we left the premises.

This work was not exactly what I'd had in mind all those years ago when I set out to dance professionally, but I had to admit I enjoyed it. The Crazy Horse Girls were featured in *Elle* magazine and filmed for a movie and some of us were offered heaps of money to do occasional private shows. For the opening we wore black G-strings, with straps that zig-zagged across our bodies and up around our neck. We wore thigh-length red leg warmers, black boots with solid silver heels of varying heights depending on how short or tall you were (we all had to look the same height) and a silver Glomesh cap under which our hair was tucked. The black curtains opened to a line-up of beautiful bottoms all moving in sync and lit up with spectacular lighting of dots and squares and stripes. It was simple, yet effective. Another routine displayed three girls, Grecian-style goddesses, completely naked except for a white plaited wig falling into the curve of their backs and coming to rest above their buttocks. Arranged on a device that rotated slowly, their graceful arm movements encircled each other suggestively without touching. Soft lighting and music obscured their nudity. Audiences were entranced. For some routines we wore white or pink short, blunt-cut, fringed wigs (a look that has been done to death ever since) and for the finale we swung and lurched suggestively around poles miming seductively to 'We are the Girls from the Crazy'. I loved it at the Crazy. We were everyone's fantasy up there; it was fun, sexy—and it paid great money.

Daniel loved me working at the Crazy Horse too; the whole concept of the place turned him on and he liked the kudos attached to it. Some nights he surprised me at the stage door after work. I'd find him waiting in the car for me to appear and then we'd swing by some chic eatery for a late supper of escargot or *des huitres* and champagne with his business acquaintances, and their wives and clients, who were intrigued and nervous to meet a Crazy Horse girl.

My allure—imagined or not—made him paranoid, though, and he went to painstaking extremes once again to explain to me how I was supposed to behave in company. I was to repel charming men and remain indifferent if they bragged about their Swiss bank accounts or their fruitful business enterprises. I thought he was being ridiculously over the top but he pressured me to watch every word I said and to be mindful of every gesture I made. I practically couldn't look sideways without his alarm going off. He was jealous and possessive, something I would come to realise was more about his infidelities and his own insecurities than my behaviour. Yet I didn't dare disobey; he had trained me well. I liked the male attention but I never considered crossing the infidelity line, ever. And there was a double standard going on and that pissed me off. While I was to remain strictly within the boundaries he set, Daniel flirted outrageously. He dazzled the other Crazy Horse girls with his charm and wit—and, of course, he had the cocaine they all wanted. From time to time, without even consulting me, he invited them to join us.

'Come with us and do a little coca,' he'd say with a wicked grin. He was the all-time irresistible bad boy but his flirtations really angered me; it was humiliating and demeaning.

One time during makeup one of the girls sidled up to me. '*Tu sais*, Robyn, *j'ai vu ton mari hier soir avec un tres jolie femme.*' I tried to be cool and ignore the gossip about Daniel's shenanigans with other women, but it was difficult not to feel pain and embarrassment. I knew I deserved better but somehow he had me convinced my place was there next to him, doing as he would have me do.

The more I bought into his domination the more I compromised my own self-belief. The exhilarating highs of an evening doing cocaine, socialising, dancing and partying hard came crashing down in the cold light of day where reality was less palatable. The cocaine was distorting my perspective and numbing my pain. And I noticed unpleasant changes in Daniel's temperament; a darker side began to emerge and the coke was starting to mess with his head: his paranoia, insomnia, irrational mood swings and unreasonable demands were becoming more frequent. He flew into fits of rage thanks to his unfounded suspicions about my liaisons with other men. He demanded detailed explanations for innocent behaviour that he mistook for infidelity. He never revealed his temper publicly; it was only at home without witnesses that he exploded. If I tried to convince him he was paranoid he accused me of disrespect, of making a fool of him. If I acknowledged he was right, which I did from time to time just to keep the peace, he would slap me around, sometimes so harshly I'd fall to the floor. My face burned, my heart shrank with shame. He vilified me for humiliating him. He called me a 'whore, nothing but a common, vulgar woman'.

Foolishly, I endured it. I found a steely resolve; after all, I loved him and I had to prove that to him. Anyway I was seasoned in emotional warfare. My parents fought bitterly all through their marriage. Violent outbursts were repeatedly forgotten with a 'kiss and make up' routine the next day. My own father whipped me when I was eighteen years old on our living room floor.

'You're a whore, just like your mother,' he'd yelled with fury. He was enraged with her for finally divorcing him, infuriated with me because I was feisty and stood up to him and defended my mother. When my boyfriend Gary had confronted him about his abuse, my father descended upon our house incensed and out to crucify me. He slashed me over and over again, breaking my skin until little blood vessels burst while my sisters hovered crying, and begging him to stop. With Daniel I was unwittingly re-living behavioural patterns I had learnt in the emotionally unhealthy environment of my childhood.

In the bedroom cocaine was charging his fantasies, which he wanted me to act out. He persisted with desires for a ménage a trois, which he convinced me I should do if I loved him. It's true,

I enjoyed the wild abandon that comes with the stimulation and arousal of cocaine but his demands were getting more and more bizarre. So, plied with coke, I mustered the courage and acted my way through sex with a woman. But my attempts to satiate his desire backfired miserably when, unable to contain himself, he ejaculated prematurely. He couldn't get over the humiliation of that and blamed me. In the cab on the way home he taunted me about it; frightened me with a scary, irrational look in his eyes. I'm sure that madness came over him—cocaine madness. When we got back to the apartment, he yelled at me, 'You stupid fucking whore!' and threw me back onto the bed hitting me hard and striking my face until I blacked out completely. I woke up to him frantically slapping my face, panicked that I was not going to wake up at all. I must have been out for several seconds. I couldn't recall a thing but when I realised what had happened I broke down and burst into tears from the stress of it all.

Another time he was so sure I was betraying him and deliberately making a fool of him that he kicked me to the ground, booting into my leg until wailing sobs overtook me. I was so badly injured I had to take time off work from the Crazy. I couldn't walk without crutches for a week; he was so out of control he even accused me of flirting with the doctor who came to our apartment to see to my injuries.

It was exhausting and emotionally draining but the worst of it was I actually believed I could somehow endure it. Deep down, I was ashamed of myself for readily accepting his deficient love. The following day, without fail, he became apologetic and loving, racked as he was with guilt. He would strive to put things right and overcompensate by showering me with expensive gifts and things would settle back down for a while. A semblance of normality returned as if nothing ugly had transpired at all.

I came close to calling my mother to tell her about what was going on but I was unable to do it. I wanted to tell her my heart was aching and tired, that Daniel was a womaniser and that he left me alone a lot. Perhaps I wanted her to plead with me to come home but I feared the unearthing of the reality of my life. And my vision of home as I remembered it was not rosy anyway. Showing emotional support had never been her strong suit; a 'buck up' quip was about the extent of her empathy, and her lack of patience and understanding when it came to delicate issues always ended up making me feel worse. She wasn't nasty or uncaring; that is just the way it was. And the time elapsed since we had seen each other had created a void, an emotional distance I didn't know how to bridge. I'd left home a long time ago and she too had moved on, living a life I knew little about. So I clung to my intimacy with Daniel as evidence of his love, I deferred my needs so his could be met and I took the pain as if it was a triumph.

☉☉

At the Crazy, I had begun rehearsal for the pas de deux, a steamy and suggestive routine with another woman. We wore halter-style beaded costumes—hers black, mine white—and the threads of beads fell voluptuously into the curves of our bodies as we moved. When I turned up to rehearsal with bruises on my leg I saw alarm and pity in the dance captain's face. I tried to shrug it off as nothing when she questioned me about it, but without telling me her intentions, she went ahead and paid Daniel a visit; Bernardin sent her. I thought Daniel would freak out about that and I fretted he might be enraged with me. Surprisingly, he was humbled instead. Maybe he was shamed into it. He toned down his behaviour and recognised that he was out of control. He could see I was hurting and he tried to reassure me that everything would be alright but sadness overcame both of us. I grew wistful about home and, as if to mirror my state of mind, the season changed; Paris was getting cold again. The trees were barren and a bitter wind cut its way down the avenues. I remember transferring my gaze from the bleak scene out the window to Daniel lying on the bed reading *Newsweek*. He filled every minute of my life. Surely love was not meant to be this tragic? I longed for the salty sting of the fresh ocean air of home; the cacophony of birdlife, the early-morning call of kookaburras, warm, sunny days, sarongs and bare feet. I'd left Australia yearning for adventure and excitement and by golly I had found that but I'd travelled way off course and now I missed the simple beauty of life at home.

22

J was finally edging towards making a change to the direction my life was headed. The emotional roller-coaster we were riding had worn me down. I hadn't made any definite plans and was not sure exactly what my next move was going to be but, before I had a chance to even contemplate that, fate chose for me. For the first time ever, I missed my period then I missed it again a month later. When I told Daniel about this he seemed unfazed, pleasantly surprised even. I desperately needed a change of environment in which to gain a clearer perspective, so flying home seemed like the only sensible thing to do. I continued on at the Crazy for several more weeks then I called my mum to tell her of my imminent arrival. Daniel booked and paid for my flight and then I was off.

It wasn't until the plane flew over Sydney that I realised how much I had missed the place. Qantas flights from Europe always arrived early in the morning, my favourite time of day. The sight of endless coastline, of gentle waves rolling onto sandy beaches, of vast bushland and Sydney Harbour cast in a blazing dawn glow of orange sun creeping up over the horizon was magnificent. I'd forgotten how staggeringly beautiful it was.

Life on the Peninsula had changed, though, and I wasn't prepared for that. Time had marched on and that saddened me; friends were moving away, marrying, having babies, settling down into suburban blond-brick homes, or completing tertiary degrees. What used to be our family home was now a rental property. My mum and her partner, John, were living together in a new house; they had a life of their own. Everyone noticed I spoke and dressed differently and they paid me out about it too. I was on home turf again but I felt like an outsider.

When the doctor confirmed my pregnancy, excitement surged through me, followed closely by apprehension. It had not been a planned pregnancy but I wasn't shocked at the prospect of becoming a mother, just cautious. My sister Jools accompanied me to the doctor's for moral support so she was the first to hear the news and gave me a wonderful hug and encouraging words. I called Daniel as soon as the hour permitted and was so relieved he was happy with the news too. I didn't bother telling my father; I expected him to explode and berate me. During the few days I stayed with him and his young wife in Canberra

I kept my pregnancy to myself. I was only there because he'd summoned me.

Telling my mother was a different matter; I was sheepish and embarrassed. Thinking back, it was unreasonable to expect her to be happy with my news; after all, she had never met Daniel and had only heard snippets of the unconventional lifestyle I'd been leading.

'Well, you had better stop smoking then,' she grumbled as she wiped down the kitchen bench. And that was that. She knew from her own experience as a young woman pregnant out of wedlock that this news meant my future had been reshaped and altered forever. Perhaps she was sad, disappointed or ashamed that I had gotten myself into this situation or maybe she didn't care but, standing there against the kitchen door, I felt silly and insignificant. I'm not sure what I wanted from her, I just know I wanted more: at least a show of affection, of love and support. Even a discussion about my options would have been good, but she didn't deliver. I don't believe she gauged just how scared I was but, then again, I had always been so clever at disguising my fear; how could she possibly have known?

People, especially my mother, always assumed I was confident, streetwise, intelligent and savvy but that was a lot to live up to and for the most part was an inaccurate assessment of my emotional maturity. I really needed my mother at this time but I realised she—and my father, for that matter—were never going to be the parents I wanted them to be. I felt completely alone and consumed by a dreadful sense of loss and wanted only to retreat into the familiarity of my comfort zone with Daniel. I flew back to Paris.

My baby bump didn't show until I was about five months and, to my great relief, Daniel toned down his outrageous life-style, proudly showing me off and announcing our good news to everyone. We took off to the French Riviera for the summer, spending most of our time in Saint-Tropez. We stayed in a rambling house high in the hills with one of Daniel's associates who'd lived most of his life in the United States and who retreated to the Riviera for the summer season with his wife.

With my tummy growing fuller every day, Daniel and I spent our time swimming and lying in the sun on our beach beds, playing chess and taking lunch with our hosts in busy beachside restaurants. Late afternoon we wound our way back up to the house, the boys racing their prestige cars around murderously sharp curves along the narrow road that cut its way through steep hills.

Those months were for the most part sheer bliss. I was primed with hope and dreams about my baby and our future. It was summer and we were on the French Riviera, cruising up and down la Cote D'Azur in an open-top sports car. Our spirits soared in the holiday atmosphere of warm sunny days, balmy evenings and cool Mediterranean waters. Everything was going to be alright after all. Daniel fussed and crooned over me like I was a delicate piece of china, happy and proud at the prospect of fatherhood.

We shopped for practical Italian leather sandals and elegant flowing dresses so I would be comfortable. We got lost in plans for our future, talked for hours about our son—Daniel expected a son—and the life we would give him.

But soon enough the novelty began to wear thin for Daniel. My greatest fears were realised when his old habits slowly crept back in. He started to leave me at home alone at night, while he took off to be among the festivities, the women and the cocaine. His moods began to alter again, swinging from caring, attentive partner to frustrated and annoyed bachelor. I could feel his resentment soar whenever I got in the way of his social activities. I endured it until I could no longer play this game with him. I had my baby to think of; I wanted to go home to my mum and, on the doctor's advice, I flew home at seven months pregnant.

At first I was billeted on the couch at my little sister's weather-board house overlooking Pittwater until my brother Frank offered me a room in his big stone house at Bilgola Plateau. It was a shared rental place set against a lantana-covered escarpment amid thick native gums and bush. A fireplace dominated the living room, which had 180-degree views of the beach. As the last of brisk spring days warmed into summer I walked along the headland past the water tanks and down the track into Newport Village. Eventually, Mum and John rallied and had me come home to their place.

My son was born on 20 January 1979 at 8.12 am at Mona Vale Hospital. He arrived late, a frustrating habit that would stay with him for years. It was a long and painful labour, but my best friend, Jo, stayed on to hold my hand throughout. Just as well: I could never have anticipated nor endured the agony and distress of labour without her. At one ridiculous moment I decided I didn't want to do it anymore; I wanted to go home. I knew then why women are inherently blessed with a high threshold of pain and why it is called labour: it's hard, painful work. I had to remind myself that this is what women do and have been doing since time began. I told myself no matter how unbearable the pain, it would eventually end. And so it did. After 24 hours of labour, Danielito finally emerged with peeling skin and long fingernails. His little crown of thick black hair lay parted straight down the centre of his head and his liquid dark eyes looked all about, serene and calm as he cruised into the world. As he nestled in the crook of my arm, suckling his first drops of mother's milk, any memory of pain vanished and was replaced with sheer joy and overwhelming love. From unfathomable depths within me came an inner peace. I would nurture and love and care for this child. I found a higher reason for being and a sense of purpose like never before.

Those first six weeks after delivery were perhaps the most enjoyable time I can remember with my mum—ever. She was full of practical solutions to quiet a disgruntled child. Her simple, commonsense advice about the virtues of breastfeeding and a sound routine to make both mother and baby happy came from her own strong maternal instinct. She was a natural, and with her guidance I too felt like a natural: I took to parenting easily and instinctively. When it came time to return to Paris I was confident and relaxed about mothering, happy to launch into the next phase of life with Daniel and my beautiful child.

23

I flew back to Paris in the early autumn leaving behind bright days and perfect blue skies. The oppressive humidity of summer had eased and everywhere leaves were turning gold. I secured Danielito firmly in a cloth baby carrier, which was close to the warmth of my plentiful bosoms and the comforting sound of my heartbeat and conveniently freed up both my hands. At six weeks he was still so tiny. We had a big journey ahead and, in the days leading up to our departure, I contemplated how different life would be on the other side of the planet, on my own with my new son, without backup from my mum.

At Charles de Gaulle I descended the escalator into arrivals, anxiously scanning a sea of expectant faces but my heart sank when I couldn't see him. I chatted to Danielito, reassuring him that Daddy would be here soon and patted his back as he sat snugly into my chest, his eyes watching mine. As the minutes ticked on, anger and frustration surpassed my disappointment. I paced up and down that terminal wondering where the hell Daniel was and sat there deflated, clutching my new baby as I watched other families and loved ones greet, embrace and then leave. About 30 minutes had passed when an announcement rang out from overhead summoning me to the information desk where finally he appeared, in the wrong spot but, nevertheless, there he was, his brother Chiqito trailing behind.

No matter how infuriating Daniel's cavalier attitude, I could never stay angry with him for long. His beaming face and jubilant mood upon seeing his son brought tears to my eyes. Together as a family for the first time, we bundled Danielito into the car and sped off along the Périphérique, heading for home.

Chiqito was staying with us for a while. He didn't speak English so we conversed in French. Chiquito was the complete opposite of his brother: while Daniel was gregarious, outgoing, playful, curious and amusing, Chiqito was introverted, sulky and intense. He moped about, which gave me the spooks, and he looked like one of Che Guevara's gang with his beard and olive green army jacket. His trademark South American Latin machismo incensed me. At home, he sat around expecting to be waited on hand and foot. I tolerated it for a while, after all he was family now, until one evening during dinner he demanded, 'Robyn, where is the milk!'

He glared at me as though I was an imbecile because I had neglected to serve him his milk. I stopped eating, looked up and scowled back at him. Then, seething with resentment, I marched off to the kitchen, poured a glass of milk and returned to the dining table.

'Milk, Chiqito? Did you want milk? Here is your fucking milk, Chiqito!' I said as I flung the glass at him, showering him with its contents. He was astounded that I had the audacity to humiliate him and as he stood up indignant and angry with milk dripping everywhere, Daniel suggested he go out for a while.

Life ambled on. I adored being a mother and immersed myself in the joy of my son. He was a happy baby, content and compliant, and he filled me with so much happiness—I never knew I could love so much. Soon enough I got back into classes at the Clichy Studios, where I picked up information about an audition for a TV variety show with Antenne 2 for a prime-time slot. Six dancers were needed for a one-off program for a popular comedian and celebrated TV personality. Danielito was still very young but this was only a week's work so it was doable if I could rely on Daniel for support. I arrived at the audition with Danielito in the pram and there were hundreds of dancers, a cattle call of hopefuls warming up. What a nightmare. I didn't have the time to wait my turn; I had to audition sooner rather than later so I could get my child home, fed and down for a nap. Darting my eyes around the room I sized up the situation, trying to decipher who was who and decided to make a bold move. I made my way up front, steering the pram through the crowded room, in and around indignant, grimacing dancers. It must have been interpreted as arrogance by the other dancers but not so the choreographers, who, after hearing my brief explanation, asked me to take my place. '*Bien sûr, allez prenez votre place, s'il vous plait.*'

As trim as ever in my jazz pants, all made up and my hair in a high ponytail, confident about my ability, I had no compunction about jumping the queue. I took my place in a line of four others, strutted my stuff and, much to the chagrin of the other dancers who had been waiting for hours, I was offered the job immediately. Rehearsals would start the following week at the studios of Antenne 2. I packed up my baby, hailed a cab and headed off home with my exciting news.

I was happy to have made the audition and glad at the prospect of working again but I did worry about Daniel's reliability. I managed to pin him down to explain my need for him to look after Danielito for the week's rehearsal period and I thought he understood. I believed him when he agreed to be supportive but to my absolute astonishment the very first morning of my rehearsals Daniel was absent. He had been out all night and that morning I paced up and down the apartment, praying for him to arrive but worried that even if he did show at the eleventh hour, he would not be in a fit state to babysit. I was angry with him and frustrated with his selfishness and disregard for me.

While I was stressing about where he was and who I could call for childcare, a girl phoned wanting to know Daniel's whereabouts. She prattled on and on but I understood immediately by her tone that she was an 'other woman'. Daniel had let her down; he had kept her waiting too. Not that I really gave a damn—I knew what he was like. At first I was indignant with her but in a split second I decided to use her vulnerability to my advantage. I told her that Daniel would be back soon, and that I was desperate for a babysitter. I'd met her briefly once before and knew her to be of sound character: she was an English girl working as a journalist in Paris and obviously smitten with Daniel. I also knew she'd agree to babysit for me because she would be most certainly hoping to run into him. It was devious of me, I know, but I was going to make that rehearsal no matter what.

Daniel's cocaine-fuelled social life continued enthusiastically. Occasionally I stepped out myself, taking the opportunity to break my routine and really let my hair down to party with friends. I found babysitters at the local laundromat, where I ran into American and English backpackers who were more than happy to make some cash childminding. I always made sure Danielito was fed, bathed and tucked in bed asleep before I left and I always knew when to call it a night, even if Daniel didn't. My social appearances were fairly infrequent, so I was greeted with enthusiastic embraces from friends and the Colombian crew, who were glad to see me out and about. I was given due respect from smiling people, some of whom had only heard about me as 'Daniel's woman', people who had rarely seen me and probably wondered what sort of woman could live with a man like Daniel. It felt good to be among it all again but it was impossible to ignore the female attention Daniel drew. I told myself their flirtations were unprovoked or their glances, when they thought nobody was watching, were harmless. But I was never quite sure what had transpired between him and these flirty glamourpusses or how intimate he had become with these women.

Mostly though, Daniel's late-night rendezvous meant that I spent a lot of time alone with my son. He wasn't exactly a hands-on father. I tried to rationalise his behaviour and told myself it was just the way he was, and there was no relationship without compromise. But no matter which way I cut it, deep down I was troubled about his infidelities and I resented the fact that I was the one making all the compromises.

That summer we headed south again. I was so glad to get out of the grime and cold shadows of Paris, to be away from nightclubs and seedy people. The change of air was exhilarating for all of us and, happy to be with my family, just the three of us, I left my woes behind. Daniel's loving, protective self reemerged and Danielito had his first swimming lessons in the warm Mediterranean waters. He gleefully complied when I taught him to blow out as we submerged and to breathe in as we surfaced while his father, watching from his beach bed, proudly explained to curious and nervous onlookers: 'It's okay, it's okay, she's Australian. That's what they do over there.'

Warmed by the sun and lulled by the holiday atmosphere, life slowed down and regained some normality. It was a tranquil time, relaxing and enriching, almost idyllic. We were like other families holidaying on the coast, though having Daniel all to myself without unhealthy distractions was not the norm for us.

24

It was early morning. Grey light from the disap-pearing night filtered through the windows. Danielito and I were snuggled up in bed and at the sound of Daniel entering the room we peered up and over the bedclothes. He smiled and remarked how cute we were and how glad he was to be home. He embraced us both and played with his son as I walked to the bathroom for a morning pee. Glancing out the window I saw streets shimmering wet from last night's rain and a sweet, appetising aroma wafted from la boulangerie.

Finished, I stood sleepily for a moment, looking at my naked reflection in the bathroom mirror when a faint sound, an almost imperceptible ruffling noise, stole my attention.

'Daniel, what's that?' I called. He didn't answer me and at the precise moment I turned around to investigate, a strange man appeared at the bathroom door. I screeched and shot one hand over my crotch and the other across my breasts as he stood ogling my nakedness.

'*Ooh la la, Qu'elle belle femme! Mon dieu, mon dieu*, it's the Crazy Horse girl!' he guffawed.

Narcs! There were three of them, two men and a woman and this was another bust.

I took a deep breath, grabbed a robe and braced myself. I couldn't believe this was happening and steadied my inner nerve as I swept my son up to my hip and kept one eye on Daniel, looking for some sort of sign in his face.

They went through all our belongings, frantically and desperately, and became agitated when it looked as though their search would reveal nothing. That is until they came across the safety deposit box. I shot a look to Daniel, petrified they were going to find something in that box but of course Daniel was not that stupid; he never kept anything of significant weight close to us. While the cops frenziedly attacked that box, Daniel cued me to pay attention to it, to pretend I was nervous about its contents. I moved in closer, playing my part brilliantly. I fidgeted and fussed and deliberately hoodwinked them into believing I was worried about what they might find within it. The more anxious I became, the more eager they were to bust this little box open. So certain were they that they were onto something and so efficient was I as decoy, they completely missed Daniel putting on his shirt—the one from the night before that contained a small amount of personal-use coke in the pocket—and then sauntering to the bathroom. The moment the narcs broke the lock on the box and saw nothing but useless items, they heard the flush of the toilet, looked up and realised their folly. They flew into the bathroom just as the evidence disappeared into the bowels of Paris.

They handcuffed Daniel and I was told to dress Danielito in something warm.

'Where you are going it is cold,' the female cop informed me and with that we were hauled off to the cop shop for interrogation. Daniel was taken to a different location and as I was questioned, a slew of characters, most of whom I recognised, appeared. One by one, all the familiar faces were dragged in along with all sorts of damning evidence: cash, packaging, and scales and sifters dusted with fine white powder. The narcs must have been on their tail for months. I held Danielito firmly on my lap, careful not to acknowledge anyone, playing dumb, as though I knew nothing.

That night I was locked up in a women's detention centre after a long and meticulous search through all my belongings. The wardens were sympathetic and kindly offered me extra blankets and a bassinette for my son. It was a cold, dank place with an overpowering smell of bleach. The clang of my cell door locking rattled me but I remained calm and settled Danielito in for the night, comforted only by the fact he was too young to understand the circumstances. I lay there wide awake, listening to the haunting cries and screams of inmates in the certainty that tomorrow this mess would be all cleared up.

As expected, I was released the following morning. They had nothing on me and I knew, in the massive scheme of Colombian distribution, I was of no consequence. I distinctly remember being led out through two huge timber doors to freedom and I will never forget the look of disgust on the cop's face. He shook his head in dismay at the sight of me with my son in his pram as he led us out and slammed the doors shut behind us. Somehow Daniel had contacted Diego and given him instructions to meet me upon my release. He was to give me a wad of money, I was to take a cab straight to the airport and I was to buy the first flight out of the country home to Australia.

At the airport I repacked all our belongings and tidied our luggage. I cleaned up Danielito and myself in the bathrooms. I bought disposable nappies and supplies for the flight. At the service desk the consultant eyed me suspiciously when I pulled out the wad of American bills to pay for my flight. Then, while we had something to eat and drink, I got my head together sufficiently to call my mum and let her know we were on our way. Danielito was sixteen months old and his father would remain incarcerated for the next seven months.

25

Everyone remembers where they were when John Lennon was shot. I was on the last leg of our journey back to Paris. Danielito slept soundly in the cabin crib, I lay stretched out along four seats under a blanket. Upon his release, Daniel had sent money. The cabin was half filled with sleeping passengers and was eerily quiet except for the drone and whirr of the engines soaring us through the air to the other side of the world. It was pitch black out the windows when the captain's sombre voice came over the intercom.

'Passengers, this is your captain speaking. Sorry to interrupt at this early hour. Moments ago I received tragic news: John Lennon has been shot, assassinated outside his apartment in New York. Just repeating that, John Lennon is dead.'

I was stunned, shocked and saddened. I couldn't fathom that John Lennon was dead; that some nutter had shot him down and he no longer resided on the planet. The news jolted me out of my daze and compelled me to jump up and scuttle down the aisles to find someone awake, someone with whom I could share my grief. Since prepubescent Fab Four mania through my teens, the Beatles and John Lennon's voice echoed the sentiments of all my peers—they had been in our lives all this time. I was devastated.

After months of sunny days and beach life on the Peninsula, the weather in Paris was a bit hard to take. We woke up to dark, cold mornings and the days were short and grey and mostly dismal. We endured the exhausting routine of rugging up to go out into the snow and sleet and chilling wind and then taking off everything when we got home again. We were always warm, though. Daniel bought me a luxurious Russian wolf fur coat with leather trim; he traded it for coke or some such thing. I don't know where he found it but it was spectacularly glamorous and warm. I wore that coat everywhere and it lasted for years. Danielito was snug too in his fur-lined bomber jacket, woollen pantaloons, sturdy camel leather boots and his gran's hand-knitted woollens and beanies. We had a fashionable new address, a trendy third-floor apartment not far from la Rue de Rivoli, le Louvre and les Jardin des Tuileries. It's along this stretch of road that Robert Doisneau captured that famous romantic image of *Le baiser de l'hôtel de ville (The Kiss)*. I loved our new home, a charming open living space with soft aubergine carpet. A well-equipped kitchen inspired me to bake and, although my culinary repertoire was fairly limited, I managed to host the odd dinner party. Pete the photographer invited an Aussie friend to one of our little soirees. It turned out to be none other than Jack Thompson, the iconic Australian actor. He was in Paris promoting a movie, staying at le George V Hotel.

The best thing about our new apartment was our new babysitter, Pascale, a young girl with buck teeth, bushy hair and crooked eyes who was studying at la Sorbonne. Pascale was an academic and worked part time in her father's tabac on the ground floor of our apartment block. Any time I needed her to sit, I would stick my head over the atrium railing and holler for her. She was always available and always reliable.

This was the premier arrondissement of Paris, a fabulous shopping locale connecting to the Jewish community in Le Marais and Les Halles, the biggest outdoor markets in Paris. Cafés, bars and restaurants lined the streets below and it was in this street just outside the tabac downstairs that I glimpsed Mick Jagger in a big brown Rolls Royce. I knew it was him; through the windows I could see his face grinning from the back seat. As the chauffeur drove past I halted the pram and froze to really check him out and he stared right back at me. Back in the Jurassic era of rock I grew up listening to Jimmy Page and Robert Plant and the Rolling Stones. I was not a city girl at heart but I did have an urban affection for a place like Paris, where rock stars mixed it up with the Bohemian chic, fashionistas, merchants, artists, immigrants, the poor and the rich. This was the neighbourhood of legendary musicians like David Bowie, Fleetwood Mac and John McLaughlin and I loved the diversity of lifestyles, the mix of nationalities and the humdrum of daily life playing out just beyond my front door. To spot Mick Jagger in the streets of Paris was a big deal for me. I'd seen the Stones in concert at Randwick Racecourse with my boyfriend Gary in my teens. Mick had been out front gyrating in his peculiar sexy way. The Stones had turned up in a horse-drawn royal coach—a cheeky reference to themselves as the true British royalty—to the roar of applause. The packed stadium was shrouded in smoke and there was a pungent smell of grass from people openly blowing joints.

Winter thawed into spring, my birthday came and went. Daniel planned the celebration, a table for twenty at La Coupole, which was absolutely buzzing. The whole of Paris was buzzing because Paris Fashion Week was in full throttle. We were a very glamorous table and everyone came bearing gifts. Daniel made sure the Moët & Chandon flowed; we ate sumptuously, talked incessantly. The mood was lively, spirited and sparkled with energy. Earlier, Daniel had presented me with my gift: an exquisite handmade gold medallion dangling from a gold chain with number 24 engraved in roman numerals on one side and an ornate engraved ram on the other. He had bought it from a Saudi prince in a nightclub, using his usual bartering method. I proudly showed it off to our guests and when Daniel picked up the bill for the whole table, everyone clapped and cheered. That,

I thought, was ostentatious. Then out came the cocaine. Right there on the white tablecloths of La Coupole amid the glamour and effervescent mood of the bustling restaurant, we sniffed cocaine until our party eventually moved out of the restaurant and on to the dance floor of Elysées Matignon, one of the city's fashionable nightclubs at that time.

⊙⊙

Conducting business with his compatriots kept Daniel occupied while I happily made the most of the first rays of spring sun by getting out and about in the parks and gardens of Paris. I strolled with Danielito along leafy boulevards and together we meandered leisurely through the bewitching gardens of the Rodin Museum and les Jardin des Tuileries, where Danielito had pony rides and sailed yachts on the defrosting ponds. We fed pigeons at Notre-Dame and rested at the foot of sculptures and water fountains. Each time we crossed Pont Neuf I almost broke out in song, inspired by the musical *An American in Paris,* which features a memorable scene between Leslie Caron and Gene Kelly right under that bridge. My favourite day trip was to Louis XVI and Marie Antoinette's pad, the astonishing Château de Versailles, southwest of Paris. We had to take the metro and a short bus trip to get there but it was a magical location to pass the whole day. We wandered among sprawling gardens, fountains, fruit trees, ponds and lakes and we basked in the sun. It was great entertainment and a mesmerising space for Danielito.

I enjoyed these blissful days with my son and it was an excellent way to pass the interminable hours waiting for Daniel to return from whatever he was up to. The scent of blossoms and the hint of summer in the air were so invigorating it was impossible to feel gloomy about anything. Besides, I was buoyant at the prospect of living and working in Monte Carlo for the summer—Doris had heard I was back in town and had offered me a job. She needed someone for the Loews Hotel, a replacement for an English girl who wanted out.

It was going to be tricky pulling off a summer season in Monte Carlo with a young child. Danielito was not quite two yet and he was unsettled and needy because he was teething. His little cheeks had a dry red rash and he was grizzling. Mostly he just wanted to sit comfortably on my hip with his head snuggled into my neck, thumb in mouth, playing with my hair. Normally he was so agreeable and happy. At four months old we'd taken him to a tennis match at Roland Gaross. Victor Pecci Snr and Björn Borg were thrashing it out in the French Open Final. I had never been to a tennis match; that was my debut Grand Slam, so it never occurred to me that bringing my child was not the done thing. I heard derisive comments and noticed piercing, objectionable glares from well-heeled spectators who shook their heads in dismay at the sight of an infant. Once the match was under way, however, I realised my ignorance. A crying, whingeing baby would have indeed been an unwelcome distraction from what was a spectacular challenge between two of the world's finest tennis players. Tennis etiquette, I learnt that day, demanded total quiet and respect for the players. I hadn't anticipated any agitation from my child, he was the sort of baby who felt comfortable in any surrounding, but I was very relieved that he remained hushed throughout, mesmerised by the rhythmic pelt of the tennis ball bouncing back and forth.

When Doris offered me this job I said yes immediately— who wouldn't? Think Monte Carlo, think famous car race, the Grimaldi family, stunning coastline, a destination for the rich and famous, beaches, yachts, sun. Envisaging a summer there, I summoned those unforgettable scenes in the Hitchcock films with stylish Grace Kelly whizzing along that famous coastal road in an open-top sports car wearing Ray-Bans, scarf trailing in the wind, snaking her way around majestic, rocky mountainous cliffs overlooking the Mediterranean while being charmed by a very debonair Cary Grant.

My biggest dilemma was childcare. Who was going to babysit every day for the rehearsal period and then once the show started? I needed someone reliable and caring, someone I could entrust my son to each night. He was still so young and had rarely been out of my sight for any length of time. The obvious choice would be his father but that wasn't going to happen; I couldn't trust Daniel to be responsible and I knew he'd have to fly back to Paris on occasion, so there was no way I could rely on him. Still this was only going to be doable with Daniel's presence and even though I was earning my own wage, I wouldn't be able to live there without his financial support. I wanted so much to keep on working but I really had to sort the childcare thing out if it was going to happen. But Doris, fabulous woman that she was, had it all covered; she was so good to me, that woman. She waived the need for contracts, offered me the better jobs, the spicier parts, and then she found a way for me to go to Monte Carlo.

'You can take over the English girl's apartment and she'll also babysit your child for the duration of rehearsals,' she said in that endearingly abrupt Germanic manner of hers.

Perfect, I thought. I was rapt. All I needed now was a carer for the evening performances. I wasn't too worried about that though. I had four weeks of rehearsal time to find a babysitter and the Kiwi girls I'd worked with at the Moulin Rouge were part of this show now. One of the sisters had a son and was a single parent so I was certain she'd know of local babysitters.

When we'd packed the car up with baby and beach paraphernalia, dance gear and all the necessary bits and pieces of our life and choofed off, I was exultant. We weaved our way through the ever-present traffic of Paris, jumped onto le Périphérique and headed to the south of France.

As soon as we hit that freeway, a marvellous sense of freedom washed over me. It felt so good to be leaving the hustle and bustle of the city behind. Daniel had secured a cute little one-bedroom apartment in Le Suquet, the old part of Cannes, further along the coast from Monte Carlo. Perched tranquilly on the hillside above the sleepy harbour, Le Suquet is an enchanting maze of narrow cobblestone laneways, centuries' old apartments, quaint restaurants and aromatic flower markets. From our balcony we could see the lavish seaside resorts along Rue de la Croix, home to the Cannes Film Festival and a hub of tourist activity.

The Loews Monte Carlo had panoramic views of the Mediterranean and was, at that time, the only hotel complex on the French Riviera with an inhouse casino, several restaurants and bars, and an elegant nightspot with a dazzling floorshow. The glamorous Palais Princier de Monaco, home to Prince Rainier and Princess Grace, and the famous Monte Carlo Casino were nearby in the tiny principality of Monaco and my soon-to-be apartment was about a ten-minute walk away. I had to scale a sheer incline of what felt like a million and one steps to get there but that was Monte Carlo: everything was set up high.

In the days leading up to rehearsals, we took long drives up into the hinterland of the Riviera to Provence and spent lazy days on the beach in Cannes and Saint-Tropez. At night we dined in beachfront restaurants from where we could see a trail of slow-moving tail lights illuminating the shores of the Mediterranean.

Soon enough rehearsals started and, as much as it pained me, I had to leave my baby with Nicola, the English girl. I packed him up in the morning, took the train from Cannes and dropped him off at Nicola's before work. She was sweet and caring and had lots of experience with children, being the eldest child in a family of four. I felt comfortable leaving Danielito with her, although that very first morning I handed him over was a bit rough. I worried all day and phoned Nicola whenever I got a moment to sneak out of rehearsal just to know how he was going. The worst moment was at the end of the day when I went to pick him up. I bounded up those steps frantically only to find him bawling his little eyes out. I flung my arms around him, hoisted him up to my hip and rocked him back and forth. He hugged me so tightly and sobbed into my neck, it was heartwrenching.

Rehearsal each day was gruelling but exhilarating, exhausting but satisfying. The choreographer, Martine, was a stern, no-fuss French girl who, despite her petite frame, was physically powerful. I was impressed immediately with her clean technique and dance style. She demanded a neat, sharp, polished finish and I thrived on her choreography, a combination of strong lyrical jazz and funky moves that you could really get your teeth into. There were the obligatory fluffy, glam bits for opening and finale but mostly it was the sort of work that really showcased my talent. As always, I danced with passion, and threw myself into the moves confidently. My renewed vigour grabbed everyone's attention. I could hear muffled whispers from approving dancers in the wings checking out the new chick and I felt energy levels in the room surge. I was elated to be back working again.

Life clicked into a steady pace. Danielito settled into his new routine, allowing me to enjoy rehearsals, and I relaxed, pleased that I had been able to pull this whole thing off. But just as I was starting to think it had all worked out—calamity! Again!

We were having an after-work drink in the bar. We'd been rehearsing all day and Nicola had returned Danielito to me—he sat in his pram, disgruntled and crying from the pain of cutting a tooth. It had been a long day, my body was tired and salty from a sweaty workout and I just wanted to get home and settle my baby. His crying was starting to irritate everyone and I was getting annoyed myself, because Daniel was supposed to pick us up and he was keeping us waiting.

'Where is he?' I wondered as I bent over to pick up my child. What if he's in trouble? What if he's caught up with the police or something? It was a fleeting thought but for a scary moment my heart skipped a beat. And then I saw them: two uniformed policemen, armed and threatening, entering the bar. I continued trying to settle Danielito, hoping this was not about us. But then they turned from the bar and headed for me. My heart sank. I knew instantly it was about Daniel. I nervously patted Danielito's back, rocking him as they asked a series of questions to confirm my identity.

Daniel was being held at the local station.

'For what?' I demanded. 'What has happened?'

'Just come with us, madame. We can sort it out at the station.'

Danielito and I were escorted along the hotel's main corridor past the racket and frenzy of gamblers, drawing stares and glares from patrons curious about the spectacle of two armed policemen escorting out a woman with child. Getting into the police vehicle, I held Danielito close to my chest with a protective arm and prayed this was not going to be serious. I remained quiet and pensive during the short drive to the station, dreading the inevitable.

Sure enough, there Daniel was, locked in a cell in the back, sitting on a long, narrow bench, elbows resting on knees with his head in his hands, looking glum.

'What happened?' I asked, shaking my head.

'Nothing, Robs, not a goddamn thing. They just don't like the look of me.'

Danielito wriggled in my grasp and continued sucking his thumb.

'We have to leave, Robs. We can't stay here!'

'What do you mean we?' I retorted angrily. 'I have a great job here, an apartment, an obligation to Doris—I can't go, I don't want to go.'

Monaco is a conservative, right-wing state with a heavy police presence to safeguard the royalty who live there. Anyone who looks even slightly suspect is hauled in for interrogation. And they'd spotted Daniel zooming around the streets; how could you miss him? Flamboyant in his flashy car, windows down, a cavalier arm resting outside the vehicle and a big wide grin on his handsome tanned face, music blaring from the stereo; he was an obvious target. They were on to him in a flash. And he was a Colombian man, which aroused suspicion at the best of times. But the car, the Rolex, the expensive Nikon equipment and the Winchester rifle they discovered in the trunk set off alarm bells.

'We don't know what you are doing in this town but we don't want you to stay,' they had told him. They were serious. He had to leave the principality within 24 hours and they only granted him that time because his story about me living in town and working at the Loews checked out.

Night had fallen by the time we left the station. Driving home, I was silent and angry. Why did he have to be so conspicuous anyway and why didn't he get it that a low profile was the way to go? Daniel had no choice, he had to leave, but I now had a dilemma: I had to choose between him and my job. I was tired, my heart was heavy with disappointment and I just wanted to cry. Why did he always put me in this situation? Why did I always bet on him changing?

Sensing my faltering loyalty, Daniel implored me to return to Paris with him. He had a look of desperation in his eyes and tried to convince me I had no choice. I had to go with him, he demanded. I was his woman, his angel, his love, and Danielito was his son. But I scoffed at that. He laid this guilt trip only when it suited him. But how could I just walk away from my job? I loved it and I would be letting Doris down, which really pained me; she had always been so good to me. Leaving now would make me a deserter. There was the apartment to sort out and a dancer to replace but mostly I just wanted to stay and finish my contract over the summer, and that had him scared.

I tried to come up with an alternative plan, a compromise. There had to be a way. I could fly up to Paris on my days off or he could fly down to Nice, I suggested. He exploded with rage and absolutely would not accept it. He was not going to leave me alone—and presumably prey to handsome, wealthy men who might find me attractive. He saw too that I had grown. I was no longer happy playing the innocent, naïve young woman, willing to put up with anything he dished out, and that worried him. Motherhood had grounded me and imbued me with a confidence that he found threatening. I knew in my heart that I couldn't stay on without his moral and financial support; it would have been just too difficult and precarious. I hadn't as yet even found a babysitter for when the show actually started and, realistically, flying back and forth to Paris or Nice wasn't going to work. It would only take one mishap for the whole thing to fall apart.

The next day, after hours of trying to negotiate my way out of this dilemma with Daniel, I had to make the dreaded phone call to Doris; there was no point in putting it off. Words cannot convey my regret and despair. As I delivered the news I could feel her turning icy at the other end of the line. I knew an apology was not going to cut it and I felt ashamed. Doris was angry, her silence deafening, but mostly she was disappointed that I was letting this man control my life.

'Well, I hope you are not going to go with this man. What are you thinking?' she said. 'You know there will be no coming back if you flee.'

I tried to explain to her that it was about my son's needs but it was no use. She must have understood that as a mother I had to make this choice but as a woman I got the distinct feeling she expected more from me. I'll never know for sure, because that was the last time I spoke to her.

26

We lived in Neuilly-sur-Seine after Monte Carlo, a rather posh area just outside the Périphérique of Paris, although our apartment block was a bit on the shabby side, I thought. The foyer reeked of an ingrained aroma of traditional French cuisine mingled with a stale, musty odour that stung my nostrils as soon as we entered. Daniel must have caught the look of disappointment on my face at the doorway and fervently reassured me that this place was only temporary. Apparently he had something more chic lined up across the marketplace closer to the woods.

'Don't worry, Robs,' he said, 'I know a woman, a Jewish woman, who has a really nice apartment not far from here. She is leaving for New York soon and we can have her place when she goes.'

Up on the third floor, our apartment consisted of a large main bedroom, which we shared with Danielito's cot, a big kitchen, a full bathroom and a spacious living room that opened up onto a hazardous-looking balcony. The railing was too low and I worried it would be dangerous for Danielito until Daniel arranged to have a perspex barricade secured to prevent any accidental falls to the street below. Our life together resumed and we slid back into our familiar if unconventional routine. Daniel behaved as if nothing of significance had transpired at all, but my disappointment about Monte Carlo lingered for weeks. Having to give up the opportunity to live and work in the south of France for the summer and severing ties with Doris choked me with regret. I'd never get work with her again and I felt tremendous guilt for having reneged on my contract. I was pissed off with Daniel because he had let me down yet again but I was angry with myself too. My loyalty to him made me somehow complicit in his recklessness and for that I only had myself to blame. I had this dreadful sense that part of me was ebbing away; that I was letting go of fragments of myself and that made me wistful and melancholic.

I think Daniel sensed that something inside of me had shifted because for a while, at least, he made an effort to appease me. A glimpse of the man I had fallen in love with resurfaced and he managed to lift my spirits with his gregarious energy and swashbuckling style. He was affectionate and attentive and he tried to make light of things with hearty embraces, passionate kisses and humour. He spent more time with his son and boosted my morale with praise for being such a good mother. He even abstained from doing cocaine for a while and stayed in at night. We enjoyed quiet family dinners together and we strolled with Danielito through the parks and gardens of Paris. We caught up with friends to see the latest exhibits in museums and we shopped for fresh produce in the markets around the corner.

Then a friend and a valued associate with whom Daniel was doing business, a Colombian man named Gorge, arrived in Paris with his wife, Eva. They were an older couple with several grown-up children and together we did all the landmark tourist attractions and dined out at fashionable eateries. Daniel really turned on the charm and proudly showed off his family to our guests. He pitched us as a picture-perfect young couple with a beautiful son, but Gorge's wife, I suspected, knew things were not as rosy as they seemed. She recognised the look that other women gave Daniel and the manner in which he responded to them and, although she said nothing, I saw in her eyes that she understood the worry in mine.

One of my brothers turned up in Paris at this time as well. He and his fiancée had gone looking for me in the south of France thinking I was living and working there. When they finally arrived in Paris, I had to explain, rather shamefully, what had happened. In an attempt to present himself as conventionally respectable, Daniel put on his best behaviour and played the perfect host. I remember he took us to see *Being There* at the cinema on the Champs-Élysées, and my brother quipped that it was 'a bit of a step up from the pictures at Avalon back home'.

Daniel was trying, and for that I was grateful. I even began to reassure myself that things just might turn out for the best; that in spite of everything, he truly loved me and I would simply have to learn to accept him and his cavalier ways if we were to be a family.

Not surprisingly, the honeymoon period didn't last long. Daniel hungered for the thrill of the night. He tired of the familial routine and couldn't wait to get out there again. I was hungry myself, for the music, the social interaction and the dance floor, so occasionally I ventured out with him. We called in Pascale from the tabac to babysit, I would glam up and Daniel would take my hand and lead me out into the night.

'C'mon, my love. Let's go, Mama,' he'd demand with his radiant, confident smile.

It was exciting for me and I headed out on these rare nights hoping to recapture the thrill and magic that was once ours. But I always returned home in a state of despair. I didn't know the people who inhabited Daniel's life anymore and I was always harrowingly suspicious and paranoid about any women. I was never certain about the nature of his relationship with them and eyed them sceptically. I observed them exchange glances with Daniel from a distance and endured their patronising comments. I tried convincing myself I was imagining the worst and Daniel assured me I had it wrong. I wanted to believe him but I always had a sense that something was going on. The humiliation of it gnawed away. I had been playing happy families at home, trying to quash out nagging doubts and assuage the mistrust that was spreading like a cancer while he had forged a whole other life, one that included an entourage of flirty women.

In the bedroom, his sexual fantasies were getting more and more bizarre. He liked the idea of me being sought after sexually and aroused himself with images of me with other men. I went to great lengths to please him, to fulfil his insatiable desires. I had to invent and contrive scenarios just to keep the peace, only to endure his abusive coke-driven outbursts afterwards. One minute I was his lascivious lover, the next he vilified me for playing the role of his whore so convincingly. It was shameful and shabby behaviour driven and manageable only by cocaine.

So on it went, with me busying myself with nurturing and loving my son while Daniel was out and about gallivanting around. For most of the time it was just Danielito and me. My son had given me such a huge sense of purpose; he filled up my heart with so much joy it was almost a relief to be able to get on with life without his father around. We spent the days together in an otherwise lonely existence, usually heading out to favoured places. Le Bois du Bologne, an enchanting wood with lakes and ducks and leafy trees, was only a short cab ride away and an ideal playground for Danielito. We ran and giggled and played and we canoed on the lake and picnicked amid lush gardens in the shade of massive trees. We did the day trip out to Versailles to bask in the sun again and we meandered through les Jardin des Tuileries. I deliberately set out on long adventures to avoid the tortuous hours waiting for Daniel to get home. At the end of the day, cheeks flushed and exhilarated, Danielito slept soundly while I passed the solitary hours listening to music, watching TV, reading or playing chess with an electronic game that never let me win.

During the days that crawled past and the hours that dragged on, disenchantment about the life we were living weighed heavily on me. I couldn't understand why Daniel had demanded so fervently I return with him from Monte Carlo if he was only going to resume his despicable habits. He would saunter in some mornings with a big grin on his face and greet us as if everything was as it should be: 'Hey, Robs, I'm home, my love.'

I was livid about his blatant disregard for my feelings and infuriated that he made no attempt to apologise or to explain himself. My frustration at his unwillingness to make any changes ignited emotional outbursts from me. I was hurting and strung out from the stress. His son was missing out, Daniel was missing out on his son, yet he coolly continued to do exactly as he wanted. Daniel didn't care and for the first time I felt foolish that I had fallen prey to such a powerful romantic infatuation with him. I saw him now as an arrogant, selfish man. My life had become totally beholden to his needs and I resented it. Perhaps it had always been that way and I hadn't noticed my gradual slide into submission nor registered my tacit acceptance of his deficient love. Somewhere along the way I'd grown accustomed to the habit of forgoing my own needs to accommodate his irresponsible ways and I had ceased to believe in my own value and deferred to his superiority.

When I look back at this time in my life, I see that forgiveness came too easily. I felt it was my duty to withstand him; at the very least, he had brainwashed me into thinking so. I clung onto him as though my life depended on him. It was a confusing time for me when a deep-rooted belief that somehow I deserved his punishing treatment vied with surges of confidence and bursts of determination to emerge from this relationship intact.

In the months that ensued, the void between the life I wanted with him and the life that I actually had, become increasingly apparent. I saw the harsh truth of it and could no longer rationalise a relationship that was unravelling from repeated humiliation and unfulfilled promises. We rarely spoke of it openly, but I knew in my heart it was only a matter of time before I had to get out and make a better life for myself and my son. Daniel knew it too. He looked at me from afar sometimes with a wistful look in his eyes and he embraced me tenderly at the thought of my disappointment and sadness. The inevitability of my leaving with our son grew quietly. Daniel and I eased into it steadily, as though that would somehow soften the blow of such a drastic change in life direction. What was the point of maintaining a relationship I could no longer trust? I had endeavoured so ardently to make it work but I couldn't see how on earth we'd reconcile our differences.

27

In the early eighties the trendiest summer location in Europe was a little island located off the coast of Spain called Ibiza. Everyone was talking about the place and its raging summer parties, its nudist beaches, the wild nightclubs—Pacha, Space and Amnesia—and an ultra-cool new bar on the shores of Calo des Moro in Sant Antoni de Portmany: the laid-back ambience, chill-out music and divine sunsets at Café del Mar were attracting international attention. Our Aussie mate Pete, the photographer, gave us the guff about the place. It was his business to capture images of rock stars, actors, celebrities and the Bohemian chic set and that year it was all happening in Ibiza. The island had an aging hippy population too, I'd heard. They'd flocked there back in the sixties to eke out their alternative and organic lifestyles and still lived reclusively in the background of Ibiza's swelling summer popularity.

The character and charm of Ibiza sounded irresistible to Daniel. He was all caught up in the hype about the place and told me we should holiday there in the summer. I had to admit it sounded like fun but while he was enthusing about that prospect and ignoring the unhappy state of our lives, my mind was elsewhere. I was trying to sort out the logistics of leaving Paris and the probability of single parenthood back home in Australia. I dreaded having to make that final call and kept putting off making any concrete plan. I don't know what I was waiting for, some sort of reprieve perhaps, or an unexpected opportunity that would forestall my departure. Then serendipity stepped in.

Dance class was one aspect of my life I had not surrendered and with Danielito enrolled in a little crèche a couple of hours a week, I was able to attend the professional classes at the Clichy Studios. I often ran into dancers I had worked with at La Cupola D'oro in Milan, the Moulin Rouge and the Crazy Horse, so it was a great place to catch up with past work mates and choreographers and it was an excellent networking environment. After an absolutely exhilarating jazz class one morning, I spotted a tiny advert pinned up on the noticeboard about a job going at the Casino de Ibiza. With all the gossip about the place and Daniel's piqued interest, naturally I was curious, so I asked around about the Spaniard from Barcelona who was looking for dancers. I had this vague sense that this was perhaps the opportunity I had been hanging out for and the timing of it was uncanny, but after all the drama and disappointment of Monte Carlo I was apprehensive.

At home, Daniel got really animated about the news of a possible job at the casino in Ibiza and urged me to find out more. He had friends and contacts there, he told me, and he knew an Australian man, an artist who was renting out his two-bedroom apartment for the summer. He assured me that there would be no glitches this time because Ibiza was not a strict police state like Monte Carlo. He went on about the beach and the summer weather I loved so much but I sensed something else was going on with him, that he had some ulterior motive for encouraging me to live and work in Ibiza for six months. I was dubious, but as always he appealed to my optimistic nature and managed to swing me around to his way of thinking. It was always like that with Daniel: a whole new landscape would suddenly materialise out of nowhere. He always had the cash, he always had the contacts and he always managed to put us at the centre of whatever was going on.

There was another incredibly favourable coincidence that prompted me to go ahead and call the Spaniard—my mother was on her way to Europe. She and John were doing a world trip together, a long anticipated event and an exciting adventure for her. Given that she was planning to spend some time with us anyway, I could enlist her as babysitter for Danielito, at least for the rehearsal period. Since Danielito's birth, Mum and I had kept in touch over the phone. Keeping her posted about her grandson's development was always a pleasure. I never let on to her about my pain and disappointment with Daniel though, or that I had finally recognised his values were the polar opposite of mine. My relationship with my mother had always been difficult but we shared the same forgive and forget attitude and were unable to hold grudges. Life was too short and neither of us could stay angry for long. My mum loved my son almost as much as I did. I knew I could trust her with Danielito and I loved her for that.

With everything so well aligned, I went ahead and called the Spaniard in Barcelona, who, after hearing my experience, offered me the job over the phone. I was a bit gobsmacked at that; after all, I hadn't even auditioned. There would be two weeks rehearsal, he explained, and we would have to meet in Barcelona to sign contracts and presumably for him to get a visual of me. Daniel decided we'd drive to Barcelona from Paris and from there the car ferry would transport us across to Ibiza.

So, off we went. Daniel was rapt about the arrangement; it was an exciting summer destination and with me settled into an apartment and organised with a job, it was a comfortable compromise for our ailing union, I thought. We could leisurely ease into our looming separation and get used to it gradually, although I suspected the bevy of beauties and the party scene of Ibiza were the real drawcard for him. He planned to travel back and forth to Paris when necessary, which suited me just fine. There was a time when his paranoia, jealousy and possess-iveness would have prevented him from leaving me alone in another country but he had either convinced himself of my total subservience to him or he didn't care anymore. For me, Ibiza was an opportunity to find my feet again, to reconnect with myself away from our highly dependent and tumultuous relationship. It would have been insufferable staying on in Paris the way things were between us but to be working again and to be living partly independently in such an agreeable location charged me with a renewed enthusiasm about life.

Our two-bedroom apartment turned out to be bright and breezy. It had black and white–tiled floors and floor-to-ceiling windows opening up onto balconies overlooking a big plaza just up from the hub of activity at one of the main ports in Ibiza. The supermarket where I would buy bottled water and gas bottles for cooking was located at one end of the plaza. There was always a long queue of locals waiting to be served and the deli section reeked of smelly cheeses and cured meats. Directly opposite our apartment, the old Carthaginian city towered over the port and a maze of terraced lanes and alleys lined with quaint houses sat on the rocky headland.

As soon as we arrived Daniel gave me a wad of cash to buy homewares. He'd paid the six months' rent up front so while he got out among it, Danielito and I set up house in preparation for my mum's arrival. When we met her at the airport, with a bit of prompting from me, he rushed towards her with outstretched arms calling, 'Gran, Gran!' It was a very touching reunion and I was glad she was with us. Once rehearsals started, Gran babysat each day and we settled into life on the Mediterranean.

Daniel thought my mother was hilarious and came home one afternoon carrying a huge case of San Miguel brew after I'd told him that she liked her beer. He plonked the case down and asked her, 'There, is that enough beer for you, Shirley?' She laughed her head off at that.

Ibiza was a magical little island covered in pine trees, lined with rocky coves and sandy beaches and dotted with white stone houses with terracotta roofs. Everywhere cafés, bars and restaurants overflowed. Sunworshippers frolicked and bathed at chilled-out beach scenes. At night, massive spotlights beamed into the stratosphere from the dance clubs, which were like huge haciendas with pools and bars and courtyards packed with hot, sweaty revellers. We ate traditional paella swelling with fresh seafood and rice, and bread rubbed with garlic and tomato and drizzled with olive oil. It was cooked on a wood fire and salted with Ibizan salt from the vast salt flats at Las Salinas. The food was delicious and hearty and cheap.

Of an evening I walked to work along the smelly harbour promenade with a couple of the boy dancers. The casino wasn't too far along but my mum worried about that and nagged me to be careful. During the day we parked ourselves on the beach, and in the afternoons I usually walked Danielito through the myriad laneways and steep alleyways beyond the doors of the old city. At dusk after rehearsals or on my day off, my mum and I would have a drink at the pub on the plaza below while Danielito tore around on his tricycle with a bunch of the ragamuffin local kids who all wanted a ride. At the hairdressing salon across the landing from our apartment I met an Australian girl who had been living and working in Ibiza for some time. She came from Tasmania and was always on the lookout for extra ways to make some cash, so she was delighted to sit with Danielito for me once my mum had left.

The show was great fun; most of the dancers were English and I became mates with Julia, an original Hot Gossip chick from the popular *The Kenny Everett Video Show* in London. Kenny Everett himself was hilarious but everyone knew about the Hot Gossip chicks; they were great dancers for sure but they were raunchy girls and wore risqué costumes to perform the unbelievably racy choreography. Julia's entertainer husband was working in Ibiza too and sometimes we'd take his purple Stag Triumph for a spin around the island. We'd roar along the dusty roads in searing dry heat with the top down, attracting all manner of attention then usually finish the day off with a swim at one of the beach coves or in Julia's apartment complex pool. I enrolled Danielito in kindy two half-days a week and, as planned, Daniel travelled back and forth to Paris. He arrived one time with his brother Chiqito and a newly acquired Zodiac in tow, which he was really excited about.

'Hey, Robs, look, my love, look, Robs, we have boat, we have new boat.'

His enthusiasm was childlike and almost endearing but he nearly fucking drowned us in that boat. He decided we should sail around to one of the beaches late in the afternoon. I didn't think it was such a good idea; the wind had picked up and I didn't like the look of the gathering clouds. I was nervous about heading out into choppy, unfamiliar waters but Daniel thought I was just being dramatic.

At first it wasn't too rough and I thought that maybe I had overreacted after all, but by the time we made it out and around the headland towards shore again, the swell had picked up. Big waves leapt into the boat, rocking us furiously, and I was seriously concerned that we would capsize trying to get to shore. I looked up at Daniel and saw the alarm on his face; he didn't have a clue. He was totally inept and unfamiliar with the ocean and I realised I had to take charge of this situation if I was going to get my son ashore safely. The boat rocked and crashed; I kept an eye on the ebb and flow, looked in to shore then back out again, trying to grasp the rhythm of the swell and how dangerous this situation really was. I was angry now that earlier Daniel had brushed off my concerns about the conditions. It should have occurred to me he was no John Windshuttle—he lacked the experience and respect for the ocean that was imbued in me by my father as a youngster and now we were in trouble. I had no intention of asking Daniel's advice, something he would normally perceive as a lack of respect and enough to send him ballistic, but he was scared and deferred to me when I demanded he do exactly what I asked.

He took Danielito then I plunged overboard. I found my feet on the sandy ocean bed and with my head just above sea level I waited there for the set to pass, bobbing up and down with the rise and fall of the waves. At what I gauged to be the safest moment I stretched my arms high above my head and Daniel handed my son over. Then, holding Danielito above sea level, with unfurling waves crashing over my face, I walked him to safety on the shore. A few gobsmacked spectators gathered around to attend to us as I staggered up the beach with Danielito hitched on my hip. Dripping wet and with my heart thumping out of my chest, I turned around just as the boat capsized to see Daniel and Chiqito struggling with flailing arms before they too reached safety.

As if that wasn't enough, Daniel was up to his old tricks: staying out all night and frolicking with beautiful women. Bastard that he was, he didn't even have the good grace to restrain himself while my mum was staying with us. He straggled home one morning with a big grin on his face after staying out all night. I was livid with him; so angry that, in a fit of rage, I threw all his belongings over the balcony onto the street below while my mother looked on in dismay. This was a defining moment of humiliation and shame for me. That he could rubbish me in front of my mother was a major wake up call and any doubts I'd had about returning home to Australia for good were eclipsed by my fury and frustration at his wilful disrespect. I'd finish my contract at the casino, collect myself back in Paris and then it would be adios, amigo!

Once my mum had departed, our apartment became a bit of a landing pad for our friends from Paris. Cecila and Veronique arrived, Pete stayed over a few times and Chiqi, a petite Colombian woman with a bubbly personality, became a close and reliable ally. She despised Daniel's despicable treatment of me and was the one and only person who ever spoke out. With her support, I was able to defy him without fear of retribution and I began to release myself from his control; to come out from the shadow of his overbearing and dominant presence.

As I had anticipated, it was wonderfully liberating to be living independently from him. I was running my own household without having to pander to his every need; without the anguish of his philandering shoved in my face, day in and day out. I regained a healthy sense of self and went out to clubs and bars with friends without having to explain my every move to him. Although he left Danielito and me alone for weeks at a time, I no longer felt lonely. I was happy to see him every couple of weeks; we were still a family after all. He was as generous of heart as always and he made sure Danielito and I never wanted for anything. For that I was grateful but I was also quite comfortable when he left again.

That summer, with my dependence on Daniel edging away, I indulged in an unexpected dalliance with another man. I'd never been unfaithful to Daniel; I would never have dared, not just because it was the wrong thing to do but Daniel probably would have beaten me to a pulp if he had ever discovered any such infidelity.

It started out as a harmless flirtation. I met him at the local laundromat, which he owned, and I remember feeling embarrassed about handing over my dirty washing to such a cute guy. It felt too personal, as though I was handing over part of myself. He was a craftsman of sorts and made wooden mobiles and seagulls that he sold at the markets. The attraction between us was instant, although I was resistant and very self-conscious for a while. But he pursued me. His persistent flirting and personable manner was so appealing, it was difficult to resist.

He lived out beyond the throng of tourists in a remote spot in the tranquil countryside of Ibiza. Our liaison was gentle, light and easy. It was so refreshing to be hanging out with a normal guy away from the drama and intensity of my relationship with Daniel. Our friendship flourished and we drew closer to each other with a touching intimacy I had not imagined I could share with anyone other than Daniel. The slight brush of his hand on my cheek, the tingling of excitement when we kissed and the thought of seeing him again had my heart aflutter. Inevitably we succumbed to our mutual attraction. It wasn't love. I knew that, but his companionship was restorative and he pleasured me so tenderly. The sense of belonging I felt in his arms after our lovemaking was nourishing. I quashed any pangs of guilt by reminding myself that Daniel was a lothario and a serial womaniser; that I had every right to taste the delights of an illicit romance.

I don't know if Daniel ever knew about my dalliance but I do remember a close call one morning when his brother discovered us together. Danielito was in kindy, his father was in Paris and my lover and I sat leisurely on the balcony sunning ourselves in the brilliant morning light when an urgent banging at the door frightened the life out of me. It was Chiqito, demanding to be let in. I came up with some feeble excuse as to why I couldn't open the door but as I was frantically trying to hide my laundromat guy in the bathroom, Chiqito burst in. We weren't naked; there was no evidence of anything going on, but he must have sensed the intimacy between us and, in an ugly tirade, he called me a 'whore, a *puta*, a low fucking woman'. Chiqito idolised his brother and despised me for what he perceived as betrayal. We had a mutual dislike for each other to start with so I was certain he would go to Daniel and use this incident against me, but to my utter surprise and relief nothing was ever said.

And so life ambled on. Summer steadily drifted into autumn, our little show finally closed and all the dancers dispersed. My laundromat guy returned to the mainland, the swarms of tourists disappeared and the tranquil pace of Ibiza was restored. Old ladies dressed in full black skirts, long white headscarves and shawls draped around their shoulders sat in the autumn sun, clustered in small groups. The howl of stray dogs roaming the streets cut through the stillness and silence and the hype and vibrant energy that filled bars and cafés dissolved.

On the ferry back to Barcelona a fine mist of sea spray wet our faces and the wind whipped our hair about. Danielito sat snugly on my lap within my firm grasp. I was subdued yet relieved to have finally accepted that my union with Daniel had failed. It had been my gravest fear for so long but the worst was over. I had been resistant to reason but at last I had an easy mind and felt mildly liberated. I glanced over to see Daniel engaged, as always, in animated conversation with a group of strangers who were captivated with his presence. He seemed oblivious to me but he must have sensed my attention because he looked at me.

How strange love is, I thought, and cast my mind back to that first encounter in Paris when we'd been irresistibly drawn together by undeniable passion. We'd had an unavoidable romance—a turbulent and exciting adoration for each other—but in the end love had not lived up to my expectations.

28

*O*ur mood was solemn in the car driving back to Paris. As the car sped on and up the highway we remained pensive, reflecting on the past months in Ibiza and preoccupied with what lay ahead. I assumed that soon after arriving in Paris I'd be packing up my son to make that final exit. I'd already begun to make a mental list of what had to be done in preparation for our trip, but Daniel, I discovered, had a different plan entirely. He had business to do in Amsterdam and he had to pick up his brand-new Porsche at the factory in Stuttgart and then, he explained, he wanted us to do a trip to Colombia. I was surprised and annoyed at this sudden turnaround. There had been no mention of a trip to Amsterdam or to Colombia and he knew I was ready to launch into the next phase of my life. I thought we both understood that it was time for me to leave, but he pressed me with the importance of Danielito and me meeting his family and insisted that we stay for the duration. I had a sneaking suspicion that there was more to his reluctance to letting us go but I gave in anyway. I was still vulnerable to him after all and I didn't really want to know if there was an ulterior motive. I reasoned that I'd hung in for this long; a couple of more months wouldn't make much difference and, besides, it made good sense for Danielito to meet his extended family. I was a bit annoyed, however, that I'd so easily relinquished my plan, for giving in again to his demands. It was weak of me to relent so readily but I was excited about the prospect of travelling to Bogotá to meet his family and glad for the extra time we'd share together, however romantic those notions were.

Daniel had lined up a fully furnished apartment in the upmarket sixteenth arrondissement of Paris for the weeks prior to leaving for Amsterdam. Autumn shifted into winter and, to Danielito's amazement, our courtyard filled up with snow. Together we made little snowmen and he gleefully tried to catch snowflakes as they floated down all over us. Paris was so beautiful when it snowed, hushed and soft and white; it made our home inviting and cosy. Our living room was filled with the aroma of a fresh Christmas tree, one that Daniel dragged home just for us. I don't know if it was the sentimentality that comes with the festive season or the challenges Daniel and I had endured, or maybe the threat of our imminent separation had him rethinking his values, but we enjoyed the time as a family. There was a comforting ease between us. I sensed a shift in the dynamics: Daniel was more compliant and deferred to me more than usual. Motherhood and living independently in Ibiza had reinforced my confidence and given me a stronger sense of myself; perhaps Daniel found it refreshing.

Predictably the few weeks in Paris turned into a few months. I had never been able to depend on Daniel to stick to a time frame; he was always frustratingly late and something always came up to thwart the intended plan. It was maddening but I didn't quibble. We socialised with the Colombians and with Eva and Gorge, and Carlos and Cirqoo, but I was disengaged entirely. I was over this lifestyle and the long, coked-up party nights. The churned-out bullshit from cocaine-manufactured conversations with shallow people who we rarely saw in the light of day bored me. I hated the way it sapped my energy and brought on a bad case of the blues. I found myself, against Daniel's wishes, turning guests out of the house long before they were ready to call it a night and I even left Daniel behind at nightclubs because I just wanted to get home to bed, away from the seedy company we were keeping.

And although I had been under no illusion that Daniel's womanising had suddenly ceased or that he had behaved himself in Paris while I was working in Ibiza, I expected some level of discretion, and became enraged about a trashy-looking blonde who began stalking us. I noticed her hovering in the shadows and lurking on street corners, watching us slyly from a distance.

Daniel had obviously been cavorting with this girl and I was furious at him for letting her get so close to us. He had probably misled her about his real intentions so I felt some empathy for her, but for this brazen hussy to appear in our lives so blatantly really rankled. I demanded Daniel speak to her; to tell her unequivocally to bugger off. He complied most humbly but the trashy blonde persisted, so when an opportunity to sort her out myself arose, I did what I had to do.

I had ducked out to the corner store, leaving Danielito playing with his toys while his father finished up in the shower. It was bleak outside, cold, grey and wet, and scurrying briskly on the way back, clutching milk and a baguette, I heard footfalls behind me. When I swivelled around and saw her right there on my tail my anger rose up into my chest. I could not believe her audacity but kept moving swiftly, eager to get inside, away from the miserable weather. I passed through the double glass security doors, which clanged shut loudly behind me, and I had just inserted the key to our apartment door when she banged angrily on the glass doors. I was absolutely livid with this invasion of my family's privacy. Who the hell did she think she was? I'll fix her! I thought. I turned on my heel, walked straight at her and opened the security doors with an angelic smile that belied my true intention. From the look of relief on her face she must have assumed that I was going to invite her in but I didn't break my rhythm. I flung the door back and delivered an almighty, power-packed punch to her face with a stern warning for her to stay away. I caught her stunned glare as she grabbed her nose, let out a cry of pain and hobbled away. We never saw her again.

Daniel thought it was hilarious but there was nothing humorous about it to me. I'd caved in and had agreed to stay on for the Colombia trip but I had no intention of withstanding the humiliation of his infidelities for the duration and was growing impatient and restless as the days dragged on. I needed at least to have a sense that we were moving forward with the plan so I was glad to finally get to Amsterdam.

It was good to be back in the Netherlands; the museums, the dykes, the clogs, the down-to-earth nature of the Dutch and the memories from previous visits made it feel a little bit like home. We stayed in a modest bed and breakfast in the heart of Amsterdam at first but moved into a big house on the outskirts of the city soon after.

A few days into our stay, Pluma Blanca, Guillermo and a tall, blond Dutch guy, whose cocky attitude really irritated me, pulled up outside our house in their flashy prestige cars. They could not have been more conspicuous if they tried and I wondered if any of them understood how suspicious they must have appeared to the neighbours. They spent the next couple of hours stashing brown paper packages into a hidden compartment at the back of the closet on the landing upstairs. It occurred to me then that my suspicions about Daniel's motives for insisting we stay on after Ibiza had been bang on. A mother and young child living in a comfy, middle-class suburban house were perhaps the perfect decoy for a bunch of cashed-up Colombians doing whatever it was they were doing. From the kitchen, where I was preparing lunch for everyone, I could hear them clanking around. I had no idea what was in those packages and I didn't ask because Daniel and I had tacitly adopted a 'don't ask questions and I won't have to lie' policy.

A few days later, Daniel took off to pick up his new Porsche from the factory in Stuttgart. He'd said he'd be back in a few days or so but I was nervous, stuck out there in the suburbs on my own, and the house gave me the spooks. It had a big kitchen, a finely furnished living area and a grandfather clock that chimed angrily on the hour. At night, after I tucked Danielito in bed, I retreated to the sofa where I sat reading *The Grapes of Wrath* and *Narcissus and Goldmund* to the tick tock of the clock overhead. Each time the fridge burped or spluttered I sat up, agitated and afraid. I had the distinct sense that someone was lurking about in that house. I snuck around nervously and opened cupboards and checked the rooms to make sure no one was there and I relocked the doors just to make sure we were safe. I don't think I had truly recovered from seeing the scariest movie of all time, *When a Stranger Calls,* and I worried that someone might be peering in from the lonely street outside. Then one evening, as Danielito slept soundly upstairs and I sat huddled under a blanket reading, I was startled by a knock at the door. I froze momentarily, wondering who on earth would be paying me a visit at this time of night, then crept quietly to the door and called out.

'Who's there?'

'The police,' came the stern reply. I stepped back, fearful and confused as to why the police would be standing on the other side of my door, then flicked on the outside light and looked through the peephole to see the warped shape of three men standing on the porch.

'What do you want?' I called out in a gruff voice, hoping to sound confident and reassured.

'We have a warrant to search the place.'

I didn't believe them and looked again through the peephole to see they were wearing jeans and groovy jackets and one guy had a beard.

'You don't look like police to me,' I called back.

They chuckled at that and then tried to convince me everything was in order, that they were indeed cops, plainclothes policemen. I wasn't convinced and there was no way I was about to let three strange men into the house without some resistance. I was in a quiet suburban street, all alone with my son, so I continued to question them through the locked door before opening up very cautiously, careful to leave the chain in place. I wanted to see their IDs and their faces and to get a sense of them eye to eye.

'How do I know that your ID is not a fake and you are not here to rape and plunder?'

They thought that was even funnier and laughed but then the bearded guy must have seen the genuine fear in my eyes and set about assuring me they meant me no harm. Eventually I had to let them in; I didn't have a choice—they weren't going away.

As they entered I instructed them to be quiet because my son was asleep upstairs. I knew what these cops were looking for but gave no hint I understood their motives. I stood back and remained outwardly calm while they methodically went through the place. They were respectful and polite as they opened doors and cupboards in the kitchen. They split up and searched the laundry and the garage and then they snooped around upstairs for a bit. I was so nervous and on edge waiting for them to discover and inspect that closet on the landing but then they began to descend the staircase. For a second I thought they had finished and were going to leave but before relief had a chance to kick in, they spotted the closet.

I stood in rigid fear as they meticulously went over what looked like an empty space. As they tapped and prodded and scrutinised the area, my mind lurched into fast forward, scrambling to put together some feasible response. I was certain they would discover the contraband. A whirling sensation gathered up from my stomach as I braced myself for the worst, but to my utter surprise and disbelief they thanked me for my patience and left. How could narcotics agents have missed the packages, I wondered, or had they detected them and deliberately left them untouched? Something was up for sure, but when I told Daniel all about it upon his return he didn't seem perturbed by the incident at all. He brushed it off nonchalantly, which I thought was foolish of him.

A few days later he locked up his gleaming new Porsche Targa in the garage and we flew out to Bogotá.

29

*T*he car bounced and jigged along, cutting its way through verdant mountains and valleys. It was a clunker, a big old heap of metal, squeaking as it swerved potholes and clung to the curves. The driver remained silent except when Daniel spoke to him. He looked too young to be driving, like a teenager dwarfed by the size of his parents' vehicle, barely big enough to see over the steering wheel. He had teeth missing and dark olive skin. This fare would pay him a handsome sum, enough for him to feed his family well and the drive would provide respite from the hurtling congestion of the streets of Bogotá. The lush vegetation reminded me of Byron Bay, only we were cutting our way through wild, soaring mountains not the tame, undulating hills of the New South Wales' North Coast.

The Colombians I'd come to know so well in Paris were all there by the time we arrived. Their kids, the cocky Dutchman from Amsterdam, Gorge, the prominent and so-called legitimate businessman from Bogotá, and Fernando Wind in his Hair were there too. The *finca*, a big old country house, sat nestled in a valley about half a kilometre from the road up a dusty driveway. We were greeted by the caretaker and his wife and after much embracing and respectful salutations with our other house guests, were shown to our room, one of several surrounding an inner courtyard.

Danielito played excitedly with the other kids, tearing around a vast living area, up and down hallways and out to the courtyard where a pond full of fish captured their imaginations. In the kitchen the maids prepared food for our evening meal while the caretaker saddled up the horses so the kids could have rides. Daniel had pitched this weekend getaway as a social get-together but when I saw the line-up of his compadres I realised it was about business. I listened in to their conversations and, from what I overheard, gathered that they had converged to implement their plan for an operation of distribution and supply. We dressed for dinner and congregated for drinks and amiable chat until the food was served. We sat around a convivial table and ate heartily of the sumptuous dishes. With the kids put to bed we adjourned to the living area and lounged on comfy couches with lama wool throws and colourful cushions. Hand-woven alpaca fleece wall hangings depicting scenes from local farms hung decoratively on the walls. The cocaine came out, so did the pot—Colombian Gold—and everyone got stoned.

I'm not much of a horse rider but the following morning I saddled up. My little sister, an accomplished horse woman and jillaroo who has been known to skin a roo and shoot rabbits, would have been proud of me. Daniel accompanied me and it seemed oddly out of place for us to be engaged in such a healthy outdoor activity together. We trotted amiably down the driveway and further on down a gently sloping road past a mountain stream gushing and splattering over mossy rocks. Curiously, for the first time, Daniel seemed vulnerable to me. He was uncoordinated and gangly on the horse and it was up to me to lead. He'd had enough by the time we got back to the *finca* but Fernando Wind in his Hair was saddled up and ready for a ride. He wore cowboy boots and a hand-embroided vest over an open-neck shirt. A brilliant emerald stone hung around his neck.

'Come on, Robyn, I'll show you something,' he called to me, flicking the reins and bolting around the back of the property. Daniel shot me a reproachful glance. He had been wary of Fernando's friendly attention to me and he knew that I found Fernando attractive. He could hardly chuck a hissy fit in front of everyone though, it would have been ridiculous, so I broke into a canter and followed Fernando up the lusciously green bluff at the back of the *finca*. I rode for my life up that hill, exhilarated and flushed with the excitement of it all until the steep incline plateaued out. I pulled the reins and brought the horse to an abrupt halt alongside Fernando, awestruck by the stunning vista that lay before me; an endless range of soaring mountains and valleys as far as I could see. Fernando shot me an intense look and then pointed to one of the slopes, saying, 'Mira.'

There in the distance I could see them: rows and rows of dense green bushes with pretty white flowers: coca plants flourishing on a steep mountain slope. I sat there speechless; the only sound the whirr of the wind cutting its way through the mountainscape. The horses snorted and nibbled at tussocks of grass and whipped their tails at annoying insects. The silence of the mountains was beautiful, almost spiritual. Fernando and I said nothing but our eyes met for one scintillating moment. I'd always found him attractive and although there was nothing in it, I think he knew. He gestured for me to follow him further into the valley but the faint sound of conversation emanating from the house down the slope was my cue to turn back.

സ

In Bogotá I was able to place Daniel in context. Far from the glamorous life of Paris, on his home turf around his family, I saw him for who he really was. Colombia is a country of gold, emeralds, coffee, coca plants and excellent pot. Bogotá is a city of contrasts, sitting so high above sea level that the thin air makes you feel light headed and dizzy. The wealth and materialism of its bustling business precinct coexist with squalid shanty towns, traffic congestion and graffiti. It is a crazy mixture of English,

Spanish and Indian cultures. Back then government corruption was rife and thieves, beggars and drug dealers thrived.

The men dominated and they had mistresses. Women played a subordinate role but underneath their façade of vulnerability they were strong, feisty and cunning. Everyone strove for status and respectability in an effort to emulate the profile of their neighbours to the north. Daniel's father, like Daniel himself, was tall and elegant. He was also stern, gruff and dismissive. He had been a high-ranking army general and witness to the bloody revolution that saw Fidel Castro rise to power after the demise of the Batista regime in Cuba. Daniel's other brother, Camillo, also a military man, remained absent. He, I gathered, did not approve of Daniel's unconventional lifestyle, especially his means of income. Their mother had died years earlier, which Daniel rarely spoke of except to imply that somehow his father had been in some way responsible for her death. There was a sister living in the States and the youngest sibling, Silvia, still resided in the family home along with Chiqito and the maid, who cooked, cleaned and generally ran around like a slave.

In Colombia you would be hard pressed to be a vegetarian. At every meal, platters of meat and chicken are accompanied by red beans flavoured with a pig's trotter and chorizo sausages served on a bed of rice with lots of pork crackling. Street vendors sell hot corn on the cob or tamales, corn dough filled with meat, chicken and vegetables and steamed in a banana leaf. The dishes are either heavily spiced with chilli or dripping in sickly sweet sauces and are chugged down with Aguardiente, which is derived from sugar cane with 29 per cent alcohol and is the country's favoured beverage, apart from coffee. In Bogotá it's cool and autumn-like most of the year and in the mountains it can get really cold and snowy, but down on the northern coast it's tropical, warm and humid with beautiful white sandy beaches. In the old colonial city of Cartagena—a maze of cobblestone lanes, bougainvillea, massive churches and leafy plazas—my conspicuous fair skin fried in the sun while everyone else turned a golden brown in a matter of minutes. At night Havana-style clubs and bars overflowed with rhumba and the steamy passion of the salsa. Cartagena sits right on the shores of the Caribbean and remains enclosed within a stone wall perimeter built way back in the sixteenth century by the Spanish, when it was a pivotal port for plundered treasures from the Indians and a lucrative target for pirates.

As guests of one of Daniel's compadres, a guy who had apparently made his first million from cocaine, we tore across the Carribbean aboard his luxury cruiser out to the Rosarios Islands just off the coast. Avocados and fresh seafood and fruit are abundant. The local kids were besotted with Danielito, not just because he was the youngest and cutest kid of all but he was a gringo and they were intrigued by his fairer skin. They splashed about in the crystal clear waters looking for starfish and octopus and shells. Watching their innocent play I thought about the strange nature of this country. Under the surface of its natural resources, its beauty and fascinating history thrives a culture of violence, a cut-throat world of corruption, drugs and money.

We stayed with Daniel's father for a few weeks but moved to an apartment complex soon after. His father was really disappointed about that and pleaded with me to convince Daniel to stay on. It was sad really; he was an old man who just wanted to spend time with his first son, but Daniel refused. We had them over for dinner though—his father, Sylvia and Chiqito—and Daniel was out to impress them. He pressured me to get the beans and rice and meat dish just right but apparently it wasn't good enough. I had endeavoured to do my best but Daniel was embarrassed because I hadn't made enough and he belittled me in front of his family about it.

We visited the impressive gold museum, which displays the biggest collection worldwide of Pre-Hispanic gold works. We took the 79 steps up Guadeloupe Hill and San Cristóbal de Las Casas next to the mountain Monserrate. Daniel introduced me to his old school mates and we gathered with his extended family of aunts and uncles and cousins, so everyone could meet his son and the blonde woman from Australia they had heard about. There were lunches and dinners and get-togethers with the Colombian crew that inevitably turned into all-night parties.

Daniel was proud to show me his country but it was a scary place. Everywhere I went I was a target because of my conspicuous blondeness. In restaurants and nightclubs, Daniel warned me not to engage in eye contact with anyone; he was certain the moment his back was turned the leering men would hit on me. Even an innocent stroll along the street was apparently dangerous. One morning I was walking Danielito to a nearby park with swings and slides, filling in time, waiting for Daniel to get home as usual. I had the camera slung around my neck, ambling along, when a man approached me. He apologised for being so forward and proceeded to warn me that 'a fair-skinned blonde woman with a Nikon camera is not safe on the streets unaccompanied. You must take your son and go indoors.'

The violence was mostly to do with the conflict between the government and the drug lords. It wasn't unusual to hear the sound of gunshots ringing out in the dead of night or disturbing wails from someone being beaten to death on the dark streets below our apartment. Turf wars between left-wing revolutionaries, peasant armies, right-wing paramilitaries and drug-trafficking gangs over lucrative cocaine-producing land were common place. In the Aburrá Valley, about halfway between the mountains and the coast, is the infamous city of Medellín. This is where drug lord Pablo Escobar, originally the son of a poor farmer, headed a drug cartel said to be worth hundreds of millions of dollars. The cartel operated in Colombia, Bolivia, Peru, Central America, Europe and the United States and Medellín was considered the most violent city in Colombia. When the United States and Colombian governments got together to wipe out the distribution and exportation of cocaine, guerrilla warfare between cartels, death threats, kidnappings and fatal attacks against presidential candidates, supreme court judges, police and government officials escalated.

After a quiet dinner in our apartment one night, Daniel sat me down and spoke to me sternly. He explained that he had to take off for a few days with his compadres; it was business, he explained, and not a trip for me and Danielito. They were venturing deep into the rugged terrain of the Amazon jungle to oversee the cultivation and production of vast crops of grass. For my safety and for the safety of his son, he assigned two of his most trusted friends to keep an eye on us while he was gone. He'd already arranged for them to take me to dinner and to the cinema and for his sister to babysit Danielito. Before he left he gave me enough cash to get us home if something went wrong and he didn't return.

I probably should have been alarmed but I wasn't. The Australian film *Bliss* was playing and I remember being the only one in the audience who laughed at the film's black comedy. I don't think the Colombians got the Australian humour nor did they appreciate the talents of Barry Otto and Jacquie Weaver. I also recall being the only blonde in a sea of dark-haired Latinos and the object of their fascination as they poured out of the cinema. Thankfully Daniel did return, although he was covered with insect bites and cuts and scratches all over his body.

The last couple of weeks in Bogotá, Daniel lived up to his lothario best and left us alone in the apartment for hours on end while he partied. As always, it was infuriating and frustrating but all the more because we were in such a foreign land. I hardly knew anyone, there was the language barrier and because it wasn't safe to go anywhere unaccompanied, Danielito and I remained holed up in the apartment whittling away the time waiting for Daniel to show up. Even up until the last minute on the day we were supposed to fly out, he was a no show. I had the bags packed, I had Danielito all prepared and we waited and waited and waited. I thought at one stage we were going to miss our flight altogether but just in the nick of time Daniel appeared, coked up and completely off his face. The next morning we flew back to Paris.

30

*T*his time we stayed in the Jewish girl's apartment in Neuilly-sur-Seine and I spent these last days in Paris saying my final farewells to friends and compatriots I'd probably never see again. Daniel booked Danielito and me on a flight to Australia from Frankfurt and the plan was to fly to Amsterdam to pick up the Porsche on the way.

The last run for home was predictably dramatic and flashy. To my utter disbelief, Daniel's Porsche was still parked in the garage on the outskirts of Amsterdam where he'd left it three months earlier. The locks on the house had been changed and there was an angry letter from the owner attached to the garage door demanding monies owed, which Daniel seemed surprised and indignant about. I was surprised he was surprised. Who leaves a brand-new Porsche Targa in the garage of a rented house for three months with no word about it to the landlord?

He managed to sort it out but it took some time and some negotiating with a very angry landlord before he could retrieve the car and that meant we were running late, again. So with Danielito safely belted in his booster seat, Daniel opened up the throttle and headed for Frankfurt at lightning speed. We flew along that autobahn, absolutely fanging it, making record time with Santana blaring from the stereo, when suddenly we were intercepted by German police roaring along in their Porsche.

When they indicated for us to pull over, my heart sank. We had no time for this; we were almost there and this last-minute hitch meant there was a real possibility that Danielito and I were not going to make our flight home. Two tall officers dressed in their intimidating official regalia of black leather jackets and knee-high boots walked around and inspected our car. I held my breath while they checked our passports and peered at me in the passenger seat and Danielito in back. At their request, Daniel got out of the vehicle for some questioning. I watched on nervously from inside the car and overheard them interrogating him. They wanted to take us into the nearest station but Daniel beseeched them to be reasonable. There was no time for any further delay, we had a flight to catch and we were already running late. Payment of a hefty fine was the only way around the situation, the cops explained, but of course that was no problem. Daniel being Daniel, he had the cash on him and, to the astonishment of the police, he swiftly whipped out a slew of American bills, counted out the exorbitant amount and then unflinchingly handed it over.

More muffled, stern words were exchanged before Daniel jumped back into the driver's seat and started up the engine. He looked at me and reassured me, 'Don't worry, Robs. We will make the flight. I took care of this fucking thing.'

I looked back at him sceptically but then to my amazement the cops jumped into their car and signalled for us to follow. Travelling at supersonic speed under police escort, we raced along that autobahn to the airport. The throaty roar of two Porsche engines tearing into the terminal entrance surprised gobsmacked passengers. Everyone was gawking as I jumped out of the car, fastened my Russian wolf fur coat, hurled Danielito onto my hip, grabbed my hand luggage and dashed for the departure gate. Daniel checked in our baggage while the police radioed ahead for air traffic to hold the plane for me. Amid all this haste and kerfuffle there was one brief moment for the three of us to embrace.

'Here, my love, here, take this,' Daniel said, handing me a thick wad of cash. 'This should be enough to start with. You can rent a nice apartment and buy a decent car.'

I shoved the cash into my coat pocket and we threw our arms around each other but at the urgent sound of a final overhead call for me to board, I let go, grabbed Danielito tightly and sprinted to the cabin door. Over the deafening roar of aircraft engines I could hear Daniel calling to me.

'Bye, my love, bye, I love you!'

And I turned at the last minute to catch the spark of his trademark radiant smile.

31

*D*abbling in smack had made him careless. By the sense of urgency in his voice over the phone I knew something must be up. The narcs had burst in while he was out, apparently, another swift and savage raid on his apartment. I knew it all too well. He had to flee Paris quickly and now he was on his way. His personal belongings, including the photos, were confiscated or destroyed. That was the worst of it—all the photos gone. The only record of the years in Paris and our life together lost forever. It made me heart sick just to think of it. He too was devastated about that and had desperately pleaded with his friend Diego to sneak back to the apartment to retrieve them all but Diego had refused outright. It was too risky.

He arrived with two Colombians—little Carlos and his girl-friend, Patricia—and I decided a few days at Pacific Palms on the mid-north coast would be just the thing. I drove them down the rugged, dusty, potholed track to Celido, a secluded beach accessed only by walking through a rainforest track that opened up to stunning headlands, big surf and miles of soft white sand dunes. Until then Daniel couldn't fathom that such a pristine place even existed. I remember the look of bewilderment and admiration on his face as he cuddled his son and remarked upon the undeniable beauty. He was accustomed to a world with population congestion, the ugliness of war, poverty and a cut-throat culture yet, here, he was awestruck by the unbelievably breathtaking natural environment.

We had been living separate lives for the past three years but letting go and moving on had not been as easy as I had originally hoped. I'd thrown myself with gusto into providing a safe and comfortable environment for Danielito. I was happy and relieved to be home again but it had taken some time for me to reacquaint myself with the slow, casual pace of life in Australia. After the sheer drama and glamour of life with Daniel, the laid-back Aussie culture seemed parochial, although all the travelling I'd done had imbued me with a renewed appreciation and respect for a country as beautiful and blessed as ours.

I'd tried dating other men—decent, stable, handsome men— but I couldn't find my comfort zone with any of them. They were strangers to me; I feared the intimacy and was reluctant to bring another man into my son's life. I was working and had enrolled part time in a university degree course; I'd made a huge effort to establish a new life without Daniel but somehow I remained inextricably connected to him. I didn't want it to be so but there it was.

Daniel occupied a permanent space in my head and he too clung on, defiantly, refusing to relinquish his connection to us. He phoned regularly, usually at an ungodly time of night and he made sure we had the means to live comfortably. He'd flown us back to Europe for a holiday and he had made the long-haul flight Down Under a couple of times now, usually bearing gifts, including a 1.25 carat yellow teardrop diamond, an antique terraced ring with 31 tiny diamonds and a Rolex Oyster. There had been a trip to Bali and with one of his generous bank deposits I'd bought a block of land up the coast, got my owner-builder licence and built a house on it.

Business had obviously been flourishing but I realised that his sudden and unexpected arrival this time was not about his need to be with us; Daniel was in real trouble. He was on the run. We were living in Balmoral in a third-floor apartment just up the road from the beach. When he arrived I immediately sensed something in him had shifted. There was an urgency and restlessness in his manner. He was impatient and on edge. Then one morning I saw it in his eyes: that unmistakable glaze of heroin. He'd been out all night and had arrived home driving an olive green Porsche he'd picked up somewhere in his nocturnal travels. He'd swapped it for cocaine or some such thing. I thought back to when I'd seen him doing *base* in Paris, a potent form of cocaine smoked from a little pipe. I'd tried it a couple of times myself but recognised it as dangerous stuff and stayed away. It catapulted him to a euphoric and frenzied high that made him absolutely crazy and wild eyed and he could only temper it by sniffing or smoking heroin.

When I saw those eyes, I understood why he was here and was aghast and heavy of heart. I never thought he would succumb to smack. But it had got him in the end, as it always does, and it had dulled his judgement. He'd lost the plot and we were his only refuge from a life that was finally unravelling. It was only a matter of time before they caught up with him—and they did, in a hotel room in Double Bay, a chic eastern suburb of Sydney. They nabbed Carlos too. Incarceration at Long Bay Gaol followed.

The narcs had apparently been tailing Daniel for months, years even. It probably went all the way back to that weird visit from the cops to the suburban house in Amsterdam and the massive operation from Colombia. They got him in his hotel room and hauled him off. I'd been there with him a couple of nights prior and only narrowly escaped getting caught up in the whole sordid affair myself. He was smacked out and unrecognisable to me and there had been a couple of dubious characters lingering there. I remember wanting to get back home to my son; I'd left him with my mum for the night and I felt enormous guilt for doing a bit of coke and for being out so late. I hadn't done cocaine since I'd returned home; I hadn't needed to and didn't miss it, but I fell into the old routine without thinking about what had transpired since, or how life had changed for all of us.

It was sad to see Daniel so fucked up and I knew that it was all over for him. He must have known too because before I left that night he gave me a briefcase with all the money in it and told me to guard it with my life in case something happened. It was early morning when I finally left and hailed a cab and, in anticipation of the restlessness and angst that always came after doing cocaine, I took something to help me relax but it zonked me out completely. I remained slouched in the back of the cab all the way home. I must have looked like a junkie to the driver because I kept nodding off and slipped in and out of sleep. I'll never forget the look my mother gave me when I walked in and the way she eyed the briefcase suspiciously before I conked out for 24 hours in the back room.

When I tried phoning Daniel at his hotel room a couple of days later, I was told brusquely by reception he had checked out. That didn't make sense to me so I called back to find out what they were on about and realised after he abruptly hung up on me again that something was up. Daniel had been busted.

Plainclothes cops tailed me in the ensuing months. I had to negotiate with greedy lawyers and barristers who wanted to get their hands on the cash and the stash. They wanted me to take the stand in court but I refused. I didn't trust them and I was not going to jeopardise the new life I had made with my son. Daniel's bust made the nightly news bulletin and newspapers. With the amount of cash in that briefcase, the lawyers and barristers were paid off. I rounded up some friends who were prepared to testify to Daniel's sound character. I went guarantor for him and bail was granted. He had to reside in my flat, which I was sharing with an old school friend at the time, and he had to report to the local police station a couple of times a week until his trial, which would undoubtedly deliver a hefty gaol sentence followed by deportation. As usual, and out of loyalty more than anything, I went along with it, and assumed, given the gravity of the situation, he'd stick to the conditions. I should have known better.

I had no idea how desperate he was and I completely under-estimated his sense of being trapped by the strict bail conditions until I uncovered his plot to skip bail. I was astonished at his stupidity and furious at him for putting me in a situation where I was going to have to lie to the police about his whereabouts. He never told me the details of the plan, but I wasn't surprised when he didn't arrive home one night. He had prepared me for what was to come; he had to, because the police from the local cop shop would certainly be paying me a visit when he failed to report. I would have to be ready for them but I just didn't understand why he thought he was going to get away with this one.

In the days leading up to the anticipated visit from the police I jumped nervously every time I heard a knock at the door. I had warned my flatmate about the inevitable encounter but waiting for them to show was an anxious, harrowing nightmare for both of us. When that knock finally came it was late and Danielito was tucked away in bed. My flatmate too had retired for the night so it was just me and the cops hovering at the front door. The foyer was dimly lit. My heart raced as I lied to them and played the babe in the woods routine as to Daniel's whereabouts and why he had not complied with his bail requirements.

At their request I had to wake my flatmate for some questioning. She appeared at her bedroom door bleary eyed and foggy from sleep and dutifully answered their queries. Once it was all over and they disappeared down the stairs, I gasped with relief. I stood with my back to the door in deafening silence, my heart thumping out of my chest. I had played my part and so too had my flatmate—convincingly I thought, or at least the cops must have seen that we were no threat, that we were of no value to them.

Inevitably they caught up with Daniel. He'd jumped a flight to Vanuatu and somehow managed to get himself entangled in the skirmishes between the Kanaks and the local government. Civil unrest on this usually strife-free French colony was headline news at the time and there he was right at the centre of it. They hauled him back to Long Bay where he floundered for the next twelve months.

I did the right thing and hung in there until the end. I made the journey all the way to Malabar to visit him and, after seeking advice from a psychologist friend, I took Danielito along too. I endured bag searches and the occasional body search while families, friends, children and sorrowful mothers queued patiently, watching each other self-consciously and waiting for their turn to register. The air of desolation inside those cold cement walls, the heavy clang and lock of steel bars and the rank atmosphere of despair and hopelessness among inmates in the visiting yard was almost too much to bear. On one of those visits I was stupefied at the appearance of Tim Bristow, a colourful underworld character, private eye, rugby player, standover man and reviled acquaintance of my father's from Newport.

There had been a rumour floating around for years, one that morphed into legend, that my father had been the only person ever to stand up to Tim's thuggery, that he had flattened him outside of Newport Arms one night. Over the years he had made infrequent visits to our family home to confer with my father. The sight of his tall, imposing figure in prison greens, emerging from the cells chatting amiably with Daniel, no less, shocked me. But when he said hello to me in that booming signature voice of his as though it was any other day at Newport Beach, I couldn't hide my embarrassment and shame. What was I doing being recognised by gangsters and when had my life and my son's life become so insidiously littered with such a dubious bunch of crims?

With Daniel's incarceration, the money stopped. Life as we knew it changed irrevocably. Since the day we'd met, his financial support had been constant but now I worked at menial jobs and had to give up my degree course to do so. No longer could I afford an apartment in upmarket Mosman and I sold the expensive jewellery, including our Rolex watches; I didn't see the value in gold and diamonds if we couldn't eat. I continued the family visits to Long Bay for the many months ahead; I felt I owed it to Daniel. I couldn't desert him just because the money had stopped flowing. I was culpable too, in that I had been complicit in his crooked dealings, but eventually I had no choice but to move into our little beach house up the coast. Ironically our move up to the mid-north coast coincided with Daniel being transferred to Cessnock, a low-security prison not far from our coastal retreat. That meant we could continue our visits up until the end, although they became less frequent.

The months rolled on and at each visit to Cessnock the tiny remnants of our affinity were snuffled out by the knowledge that his imminent deportation would sever our ties for good. We both knew that we would probably never see each other again; that it really was all over this time, but there was no speaking of it. What could be said after all these years and what would be the point?

Soon they would fly him out and with this final departure, a decade of my life would close forever.

2014

*D*aniel has resided in Bogotá ever since. Twenty-five years have flown past. He is 69 years old now and lives modestly in the apartment his father left him. Over the years he has kept in touch by phone and more recently we have Skyped each other. He has a partner these days but still addresses me as 'my love' or 'Robs'. I get a sense that he has some regrets about the way he treated me, although he is not one to wallow in the muddy waters of the past. It took a while for him to really appreciate his son but with the passing of time and with old age looming, Danielito is gold to Daniel now and testament to what was once an ardent love affair.

Danielito is 35, all grown up and living and working in Denmark. I am supremely proud of him. He is tertiary educated, has travelled extensively, is a good son and is a lovely human being. There hadn't been a lot of contact between him and his dad for many years but as he grew into a young man—and as I anticipated many years prior—he longed to know Daniel. His first trip overseas was to see his father, which totally freaked me out. He was only in his early twenties at the time and I worried his expectation of his father would disappoint, as well as fearing for his safety in a violent city like Bogotá. They remain close although a couple of times I've had to intervene to remind Daniel that it is I who brought up his son in a country that has afforded him a more liberal set of values than those of his own macho culture.

Chiqito passed away in 2013 after years of illness. Daniel was devastated. He and his younger sibling were inseparable for most of their lives and Chiqito's passing was an enormous loss.

Pluma Blanca was kidnapped and held hostage for 40 days somewhere in the rugged terrain of Colombia. Apparently they tortured him brutally before they shot him and Fernando Wind in his Hair was gunned down in the streets of Bogotá. I don't know the details but presumably their deaths were drug war related.

Jenny, whose calling card introduced me to this crowd of people in the first place, lives in London and Diego died of cancer in his home town in Colombia in 2012.

Anne, my Danish friend in Paris, is married with two kids and resides in Hawaii. We found each other on Facebook 25 years after we last spoke. Recently I visited her at her home in the Pālolo Valley up behind Waikīkī. She is still as gracious and charming as ever. Our friendship has endured.

I also found my friend Ruud through Facebook and was surprised and delighted to eventually find him living in Perth WA.

I am in my late fifties now, with a sixtieth birthday looming. It's hard to grasp where the years went. By the time Daniel was deported, I had met someone with whom I spent the next ten years of my life. We had a daughter, Elke, who is now 22. Elke is a beautiful girl, talented, educated and already well travelled. She and her brother, Danielito, are very close. When Daniel finally left, I went back to what I love best and started teaching classical and jazz ballet and eventually opened up my own dance and drama centre in Sydney. I choreographed and coordinated charity events, staged pantomimes in local shopping centres, was invited to judge talent quests, consulted for the Rock Eisteddfod and put together a professional group of dancers. I rediscovered my joy for dance and realised my accomplishments and breadth of experience as a professional dancer and intrepid traveller.

When I think back to the years with Daniel, I see a former version of myself that bears little resemblance to the woman I am today. I don't do regret but sometimes tears well up when I remember how sublime our love was one minute and how painful it was the next. It saddens me when I think about how much of myself I let go in the name of love. I have been single for years now but ever the optimist I'm hoping for love to make one miraculous final encore.

ACKNOWLEDGEMENTS

Enormous gratitude to Rebecca Kaiser and her team of professionals at Allen & Unwin Publishers including: Belinda Lee, Lisa White and Lara Wallace, who all made my first publishing experience an absolute pleasure.

Many thanks to The Australian Writers Centre whose workshops gave me the strategies to get going in the first place, in particular Patti Miller and her Life Writing Workshop and to the national head of The Centre, Valerie Khoo, the most dynamic woman I have ever met. To Sophia Barnes, University of Sydney, whose assessment of my manuscript inspired me to keep at it and to my dear and loyal friend D whose support and encouragement helped me sustain my belief that I could actually do this.